Contents

SATSUKI AZALEA. Height: 18 inches. From Japan. About 100 years old.

CHINESE WISTERIA. Wisteria sinensis. *Height: 25 inches. At least 25 years old.*

The Spirit of Nature~ The Hand of Man

To evoke the spirit of nature — that is the essence of bonsai. What place in nature is special to you? A spot under a blossoming cherry tree? A moss-carpeted forest? A pine-studded mountain crag? Your own bonsai can take you to that place.

The first section of this book is for inspiration, to give you a feeling of the spirit of nature reflected in the art that is bonsai. The second section gives you the hands-in-the-dirt instructions that will bring that spirit of nature alive for you.

BONSAI

Culture and Care of Miniature Trees

By the Editors of Sunset Books
and Sunset Magazine

Lane Publishing Co. · Menlo Park, California

Thank You...

to the people who shared their bonsai and their know-how with us: Connie Hinds, Horace Hinds Jr., Clara Howard, Dr. Francis Howard, Alexandria Planting, John Planting, Robert Saburomaru, Toshio Saburomaru, Peter Sugawara, Kenneth Sugimoto, Carl Young, and Shin Young.

Supervising Editor: **Patricia Hart Clifford**

Research and Text: **Buff Bradley**

Design: JoAnn Masaoka
Artwork: Dinah James
Photography: Ells Marugg

Cover: Mugho pine (*Pinus mugo mughus*).
Owned by Clara Howard and Dr. Francis Howard.
Photographed by Ells Marugg.

Executive Editor, Sunset Books: David E. Clark

Second Printing April 1977

In springtime the wisteria and azalea bloom. Summer brings fruit to a crabapple, berries to a cotoneaster.

MIDGET CRABAPPLE. Malus micromalus. *Height: 16½ inches. From a graft. 8 years old; trained last 4 years.*

CRANBERRY COTONEASTER. Cotoneaster apiculata. *Height: 9½ inches. From a cutting. 7 years old.*

AZALEA. Rhododendron. *Height: 20 inches. Imported from Japan. About 125 years old.*

5

Autumn means colorful
foliage; in winter, trees
are stark and bare.

JAPANESE MAPLES. Acer palmatum. Height: 21 inches. Oldest trees from seed: 15 years old. Younger trees added from nursery: 9 years old.

SAWLEAF ZELKOVA. Zelkova serrata. Height: 15½ inches. From seed. 15 years old; younger trees 12 years old.

SAWLEAF ZELKOVA. Zelkova serrata. Height: 16 inches. From seed. 15 years old.

Your first encounter with bonsai (bone-*sigh*) may startle you. There, standing in front of you, is a tree 50, 100, 200 years old, with all the natural dignity and gnarled venerability of its age — and it's only 12 inches tall! You have the fleeting impression of being a Gulliver in Lilliput.

Your next feeling may be that you want to try your hand at the art of bonsai. Few who enjoy working with plants can resist bonsai's challenges and rewards. And it's not nearly as difficult as you might expect. All it requires is some basic knowledge of plant growth habits, pruning techniques, and plant care. And all you'll need to succeed are care and patience. You aren't going to create a beautiful bonsai overnight. But neither will it take you 50 years — look at the ages of the trees pictured in this book.

Defined simply, bonsai is a dwarfed tree growing in a tray or a pot. (*Bon* means tray or pot in Japanese; *sai* means to plant; so bonsai means literally, "planted in a tray.") Leaving it at that, though, is like defining a symphony as a collection of notes played on a collection of instruments. Both statements are true as far as they go, but there is so much more to say.

Like *ikebana*, the Japanese art of flower arranging, bonsai is considered an art in its home country and among its devotees throughout the world. Does that sound more than a little intimidating? It needn't be. Any pastime capable of sustaining your interest and enthusiasm for a number of years is going to involve challenges and even difficulties. They're the spice. They make the rewards of success that much more satisfying.

Nobody who's just taken up oil painting expects to paint a masterpiece right away. Nor will the bonsai beginner create perfection at first. But bonsai offers twin opportunities for pleasure. Along with the artistry of it comes the achievement of growing something — not just *anything*, but a 10-inch-high tree that by all rights ought to be 40 or 50 feet tall. You can experience the sheer wonder of watching a maple tree — small enough to hold in your hand — sprout its tiny buds in the spring, fill out with deep green summer foliage, turn bright red in the fall, and drop all its leaves in winter.

Whether or not your bonsai is a horticulturist's *Mona Lisa,* you can appreciate it deeply. As you become caught up in the hobby, you'll continue to strive for artistry, refining your techniques to create desired effects. And you'll continue to be delighted at the sight of a mature tree thriving in a shallow container.

The roots are in Japan

Appreciating the beauty of the natural world seems to be almost a national trait in Japan — think of the unsurpassed serenity of a Japanese garden; think of *ikebana* (flower arranging); think of the understated *sumi* landscape paintings.

Because Japan is crowded — and has been crowded from its earliest recorded history — the gardener often has had very little space in which to work. And so he has learned to capture the essence of a natural setting without exactly duplicating it. A Japanese tree garden in a postage-stamp space may create the illusion of being the center of a giant forest. A Tokyo courtyard, separated from the street by a single wall, may contain all the serenity of a mountain glade.

Perhaps because of crowded conditions, the Japanese gardener characteristically focuses on details rather than on panoramas. In Japan, to capture the essence of one tree, a grouping of flowers and grasses, or even a single rock is to bring all of nature home.

The exact beginnings of bonsai are lost in the clouds of time. Though some indications suggest that its origins may lie in the China of over 1500 years ago, the oldest surviving piece of evidence we have about bonsai is a famous Japanese scroll painting 700 or 800 years old, showing a dwarf tree in a ceramic container.

Early Japanese aristocrats displayed a fondness for unusual botanical specimens. Highly valued were the trees dwarfed by natural circumstances and weathered into unusual and sometimes fantastic shapes. Such dwarf trees were collected from all over Japan.

Wonderful old stories tell about men whose work it was to collect these trees — about the harrowing extremes to which they went, often clinging to the sheer walls of cliffs as they claimed dwarf trees growing there. These dearly-got trees were treasured — and very expensive.

To this day the bonsai enthusiast prizes above all others the tree dwarfed in the wild — perhaps a tiny pine growing in a crack of a granite boulder; a juniper in poor soil, robbed of light by its larger neighbors; or a windswept cypress on a rocky coastline dwarfed and shaped by severe wind and weather.

What happened, of course, was that as enthusiasm for owning naturally dwarfed trees spread, the trees became more difficult to find. It was only a short step from that situation to the development of artificial dwarfing.

Sophisticated Japanese horticulturists took the next step after that as well — artificially shaping the trees.

Tree shaping went through many incarnations over the centuries before it became what we know today as bonsai. At one period, for instance, the highest goal of the art was to create the most grotesque, bizarre, and unnatural shapes imaginable.

In the mid-19th century, today's esthetic principles (based on asymmetrical balance, as in a scalene triangle; see page 18) took hold. But not until 1909 — at an exhibition in London — did bonsai appear in the western world. Since then, interest in the art has increased enormously.

The first serious practitioners of bonsai in the United States were Japanese-Americans on the west coast who had brought the art with them from their mother country. These people continue to be invaluable resources for bonsai enthusiasts throughout the country, both because they are long-time masters of the art and because they are living links with the sources of bonsai.

Not that bonsai must cling rigorously to its past — the American chapters in the history and development of bonsai are certain to add new and distinctive marks. For one thing, a broader range of climates exists here, supporting different flora — desert or tropical natives, for instance, of which Japan has none.

Bonsai is practiced widely in the United States, not just on the west coast and by no means only by Japanese-Americans. Servicemen returning from Japan after World War II brought back an enthusiasm for bonsai, as have many of the hundreds of thousands of American tourists who have visited that country in the past 30 years.

Getting started in bonsai isn't difficult or expensive; it's not even time-consuming. And if you find yourself getting swept up by it, you won't have to travel to Japan to find all the resources you'll need to educate yourself and grow in skill and artistry.

Bonsai clubs abound, both locally and nationally, (see page 80) and bonsai periodicals and books are plentiful. Bonsai experts — Japanese as well as American — regularly tour the United States, giving lectures and demonstrations. In addition, bonsai exhibits are becoming more and more common at nurseries and botanical gardens and even in museums. Anyone who wants to get involved in the hobby in this country will find ample resources of all kinds.

Bonsai's beauty is ageless

The link between bonsai and great age may have wedged itself into your mind: that foot-high tree that's years older than you are. But try to shake loose the notion that a bonsai has to be old to be good. You won't have to wait around for your cotoneaster's bicentennial to see it reach a fullness in maturity and form.

A bonsai may very well be 100 years old, but this doesn't mean that the plant has been under cultivation all that time. True, there are some bonsai that have been constantly in training for 2 or 3 centuries and are veritable treasures. But many very old bonsai have spent the greater part of their life in the wild, growing in a natural state before being collected and trained for container life.

Actual age is not what's important in bonsai — apparent age is. Those valued characteristics of great age needn't be naturally come by. Bonsai is an art, and art is the human hand at work, in this case cooperating with nature, perhaps causing a tree just a few years old to look 100 years old.

There are ways to create the appearance of age — peeling off bark from trunk, branches, or exposed roots to make dead wood or scarring and hollowing the trunk. (See pages 23 and 64 for illustrations of these techniques.)

Evergreen conifers are favorite bonsai subjects precisely because, even when very young, they often give an impression of great age. Deciduous trees are more inclined to look their actual age.

It's nature and it's art

Bonsai are not exact duplicates of trees growing in the wild. Rather, they are evocations of the spirit of nature, of the life force of the natural world. They are manmade shapes that suggest nature — as does, say, an impressionist painting — rather than duplicate nature, as a photograph might. The artist's feeling for balance, form, and line combine with nature's juices to evoke a larger and deeper concept.

Viewing bonsai should be a kind of rest, a green pause in the staccato pace of daily life, a brief contact with nature's great calm. A single bonsai might suggest an entire scene to the viewer — with sounds and smells and the feel of the air.

BONSAI OAK (below) captures spirit of oak in nature (left) without imitating it. Full-grown trees can serve as models as you train your bonsai.

To develop your taste and judgment you'll have to study trees, both those in their natural conditions and those trained as bonsai.

Learn about trees in the wild by getting out and looking at them. Train yourself to recognize the conditions that make a tree grow in a particular manner. Investigate why a tree is formed in one way, deformed in another. Trees tend to lean toward water, away from wind, toward lowland. Foliage grows so that it will receive maximum sunlight. Trees that cluster in tight groves have most of their foliage high up, and such trees stand straight, most of the branches reaching up instead of out. Trees that are not crowded together usually have bushy foliage and spreading branches.

Pay attention to the conditions of weather, terrain, and soil that affect a tree's growth. Why do some trees have straight trunks and others twisted trunks? Why does a species grow vertically in one place and prostrate in another? Study of trees in nature will give you insight for training bonsai.

Through careful study of bonsai exhibits or photographs, you can also learn a great deal from what others have done. Not only is copying no crime — it's a venerable tradition for beginners and experts alike. Like snowflakes, no trees are ever exactly alike, and your copy of another tree could never produce identical results.

The best way to get a three-dimensional view of bonsai is to study them in person. Inquire about bonsai exhibits and demonstrations and bonsai club shows at a local nursery or horticultural society, and attend them whenever you can. If there's a bonsai club in your area, the members' trees may provide worthwhile examples for study. (To learn about clubs, see page 80.) In a club, you'll be able not only to see other trees but also to glean practical advice from other enthusiasts.

Many publications contain photos of outstanding bonsai specimens — they can be helpful in generating ideas for your own bonsai. The purpose of the bonsai portraits in this book is the same: to display examples of bonsai that are both beautiful to look at and provocative of ideas.

None of the "rules" offered in this book should be considered rigid. Instead, take them as flexible

Art of bonsai

guidelines for training your plants. Seldom, if ever, does a really exquisite bonsai flagrantly violate established esthetic standards. But many fine specimens show subtle deviations, perhaps because the tree itself wouldn't bend to an absolutely "correct" shape or because the artist has experimented a little. And of course, as in other arts, different experts have different standards; different teachers teach different rules.

The following pages will present rules and standards generally accepted as correct, as artistically necessary and sound for creating exquisite bonsai. Beyond that, your experience in the art will determine what principles will guide your work.

The bonsai styles

Generally, bonsai are classified according to size, attitude and number of trunks growing from a single root, number of trees in a group planting, and the kind of base the plant has.

<u>Size classifications</u> recognize the fact that bonsai may grow anywhere from just a few inches high to 3 or 4 feet or (rarely) more. You will hear Japanese names for the categories, but these names vary among experts in the United States. Here are the size classifications:

Miniature bonsai — under 6 inches
Small bonsai — from 6 to 12 inches
Medium bonsai — from 13 to 24 inches
Large bonsai — over 24 inches

The size you choose for your bonsai may depend on how much space you have for working and display. The city dweller with very limited space may choose to develop a collection of miniature bonsai or one or two small bonsai. Suburbanites with more generous yard areas, on the other hand, might be able to give a great deal of space to their plants, displaying larger bonsai.

The most common size for bonsai falls within the small and medium groups. It's often difficult to simulate age in good proportion in the miniature bonsai, and the size of the large bonsai makes them difficult to work with.

<u>Shape and attitude of trunk</u> is another way of classifying bonsai. Most bonsai fall into five main classifications: formal upright (*chokkan*), informal upright (*moyogi*), slanting (*shakan*), semicascade (*han-kengai*), and cascade (*kengai*).

Many other classifications are less commonly encountered. Some are variations of one of the five; others are styles once popular but now rarely seen. The illustrations on pages 16-17 show the five main styles and some of the others.

Formal and informal upright attitudes are by far the most common; they are also easiest for the beginner to work with because they usually require

(Continued on page 15)

Miniature:
under 6 inches

Small:
6 to 12 inches

Medium: 13 to 24 inches

Large: over 24 inches

Miniature bonsai a few inches tall make two-foot trees look enormous.

ROCKSPRAY COTONEASTER. Cotoneaster microphylla. *Height: 5 inches. From a cutting. 12 years old; trained last 9 years.*

LEFT: Japanese maple. Acer palmatum. *Height: 10 inches. From a cutting. 5 years old. RIGHT: Sawara false cypress.* Chamaecyparis pisifera. *Height: 22 inches. From nursery. 20 years old; trained last 5 years.*

LEFT: Japanese maple. Acer palmatum. *Height: 4 inches. From a cutting. 5 years old. RIGHT: Japanese white pine.* Pinus parviflora. *Height: 4 inches. From seed. 10 years old.*

TOP LEFT: Norway spruce. Picea abies. *From nursery. 4 years old. TOP RIGHT: Japanese maple.* Acer palmatum 'Sangokaku.' *From a cutting. 5 years old. BOTTOM LEFT: Accent plant. BOTTOM CENTER: Korean boxwood.* Buxus microphylla koreana. *From seed. 35 years old; trained last 8 years. BOTTOM RIGHT: Japanese yew.* Taxus cuspidata. *From cutting. 2 years old. Tallest tree, the Japanese maple, is 6 inches high.*

JAPANESE BLACK PINE. Pinus
thunbergiana. *Height: 22½ inches. From
seed. 18 years old; trained last 13 years.*

JAPANESE WHITE PINE. Pinus parviflora. *Height: 20 inches. From a graft. 45 years old.*

JAPANESE LARCH. Larix leptolepis. *Height: 20 inches. From nursery. 9 years old.*

The attitude of the trunk sets the mood. 'Formal upright' points straight to the sky. 'Slanting' seems to lean with the wind.

13

Cascade bonsai spill out
of their containers like
green waterfalls frozen
in time.

SHIMPAKU (Sargent juniper). Juniperus chinensis sargentii.
Height: 11½ inches. From a cutting. 8 years old.

COAST LIVE OAK. Quercus
agrifolia. *Height: 30 inches.
Found growing wild. Trained
10 years.*

... *Continued from page 10*

less manipulation of the trunk than many other styles.

The formal upright style has a perfectly straight trunk, perpendicular to the surface it rests on. The informal upright may have a curve in the trunk and a slight slant; the tip (apex) of the tree will be directly over the base. The slanting style has a more severe slant and the apex will not be over the base. In these three styles, the branches of the tree generally describe the outline of an asymmetrical triangle.

The semicascade tree trunk grows up out of the soil and then cascades usually not lower than the top surface of the container. The full cascade tree also grows upward first and then turns abruptly downward. In its most formal manifestations, the tip of this type of cascade should curve in toward the base and be perpendicular to the vertical center line formed by the trunk and the apex.

Let the tree itself decide what attitude is appropriate for it to be trained in — your study of trees in the wild and of other bonsai will help you understand this process. An oak or a maple suggests an upright or possibly a slanting style. Some pines and other conifers insist on upright styles; others clearly lend themselves to cascaded styles. Cypress may seem right only in a slanted, windswept style; zelkova, elm, and trident maple take quite naturally to broom style. Some flowering plants look attractive cascaded — wisteria, chrysanthemum, star jasmine, and others appear as a sheet of blossoms when in full flower.

The trunk of a bonsai may be twisted or straight. A twisted trunk is just that — not just bent or curved, but twisted like a piece of taffy. In some cases two trees (or twin trunks) can be twisted around each other.

Bonsai with twisted trunks create a spectacular effect. In the wild, twisted trunks are caused by countless years of severe weathering. They are constantly buffeted by winds, smothered in deep snows. A twisted trunk is particularly suited for such mountain trees as California juniper or shimpaku (Sargent juniper). Creating this effect is difficult, and it's best to learn the technique from a bonsai instructor.

Multiple trunks characterize another classification of bonsai. One strong, main trunk usually dominates one or more secondary trunks. Traditionally, except in the double-trunk style, bonsai growers avoid even numbers.

Certain characteristics should apply to all multiple-trunk styles. Trunks should divide at the base, not higher up, and form a "V" shape rather than a "U" or bowl shape. All trunks should be of varying heights and thicknesses. Plant the tree so that one trunk is slightly in front of the others — the trunks should not form a fan shape or a straight line.

• Double-trunk style (*sokan*). Two trunks grow from a common root system; one trunk is larger than the other. In this style, try to maintain constant proportions between the two trunks: if the larger trunk is twice as thick, it should also be twice as tall. One trunk should be slightly in front of the other, creating a sense of depth; one should never be directly in front of another, though. If the trunks curve, they should curve in the same direction. Don't place a branch of the larger trunk directly above the branch of a smaller trunk. Branches from one trunk should not cross those of another. If the trunks are very close together, you can train the branches as though the two trunks were one.

• Clump style (*kabubuki, kabudachi*). This is a cluster of trunks growing very close together.

• Stump style (*korabuki*). Here the root forms an aboveground hump from which multiple trunks grow.

• Raft or straight-line style (*ikadabuki*). These multiple trunks grow in a straight line because they are actually branches growing from a trunk that has been laid on its side under the soil and has become a root.

• Sinuous style (*netsunagari*). This tree is much like the raft style except that the single root weaves about under the soil, causing the trunks to form a curved line.

Group plantings (*yose-uye*) are composed of trees with separate root systems. For a two-tree planting, follow the preceding guidelines for double-trunk plantings. Odd numbers of trees make the most successful groupings of more than two trees — until there are too many trees to count at a glance. To create a forest effect, you'll need at least five trees.

In a group planting, the total effect is more important than the beauty of the individual trees. One tree should be larger than all the others — not to draw attention to itself, but to serve as a focal point for the eye while smaller trees play nearer the edges of vision, creating the forest effect. Because the individual trees merge with the group, forest plantings are often ideal settings for trees with defects that are too pronounced for the trees to be displayed as individual specimens. Spacing of trees should not be uniform, and no two trees should be the same size.

Forest plantings should include, if not identical species and varieties, then similar trees with similar habits and needs. The outline of the whole planting, or of groups within the planting, should form roughly an asymmetrical triangle.

Plantings should not be symmetrical, with the largest tree directly in the center of the pot; rather, trees should be grouped nearer the edges, often with much open area left in the pot, allowing space to create a sense of visual drama. To create a kind

(Continued on page 18)

Cascade

Here are the five basic
bonsai styles; some of the more
unusual ones are on the opposite
page. A description of the
basic styles starts on page 10.

Formal upright

Semicascade

Slanting

Informal upright

Literati

Driftwood

Raft

Windswept

Broom

Forest, grove, or
group planting

Clump

. . . Continued from page 15

of panoramic perspective, plant the largest trees in front and the smallest trees in back. To simulate a close-up, reverse that, with the smallest trees in front and the largest ones behind. Look carefully at the outside branches of the trees (front branches on front trees, back ones on those behind because they form the outline of the grouping. You can trim off most of the inside branches.

<u>Earth or rock</u> — which will form the base for your bonsai? Will your tree be planted in soil or on a rock? Will the roots be exposed?

Planting directly in soil is much easier than planting on a rock. The tree itself, though, should dictate the kind of base it is planted in. A tree that in nature grows on rocks in the mountains — such as a pine — will look natural on a rock base. Upright trees are most often planted in soil with only a bit of rootage showing just on the surface of the ground. Slanted and cascaded styles frequently have exposed roots since they usually represent plants that grow along rock faces or in situations where earth is washed out from around the roots.

The artist's eye--balance, line, form

All parts of a bonsai planting — roots, trunk, branches, foliage — must work together to achieve a unified effect. Essential to the effect are the concepts of balance, proportion, form, and line, as well as the appearance of maturity.

Balance and proportion depend on the location of branches and foliage, the placement of the plant in the container and variety in the sizes of branches. Balance doesn't mean symmetry — you'll seldom find a symmetrical bonsai. It does mean even distribution — for example, a heavy branch on one side is balanced by a curve on the other. The line of a planting reflects how the apex relates to the trunk; the form or outline should be an asymmetrical triangle.

All of these elements must blend harmoniously. Starting on page 23 we'll discuss individual aspects of a tree and a planting and the elements of style that pertain to each.

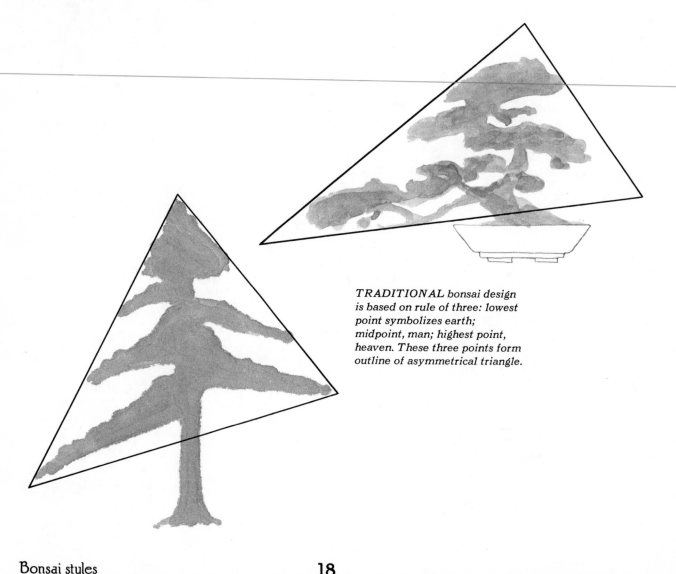

TRADITIONAL bonsai design is based on rule of three: lowest point symbolizes earth; midpoint, man; highest point, heaven. These three points form outline of asymmetrical triangle.

EZO SPRUCE. Picea jezoensis. *Height: 32 inches. From nursery. 10 years old.*

As with some forest trees, so with bonsai: a single tree may have many trunks.

COTONEASTER. C. microphylla thymifolia. *Height: 11 inches. From nursery. 14 yrs. old.*

HEAVENLY BAMBOO. Nandina domestica. *Height: 21 inches. From nursery. 15 years old.*

LODGEPOLE PINES. Pinus contorta
murrayana. *Height: 25 inches.*
Found growing wild.
Trained 10 years.

Group plantings create
a miniature forest.
Traditional groups have
one central tree and
always an odd number
in the planting.

COLORADO SPRUCE. Picea pungens. *Height: 11 inches.*
Found growing wild. Trained 10 years.

JAPANESE MAPLES. *Acer*
palmatum. *Height: 19 inches. From*
seed. 24 years old; trained last
19 years.

As mountain trees take hold
in craggy places, so can
bonsai grow clinging to rocks.

EZO SPRUCE. Picea jezoensis.
Height: 14 inches. From cuttings.
10 years old.

MUGHO PINE. Pinus mugo mughus.
Height: 10 inches. From nursery.
11 years old.

22

Trunk. Though no one part of a bonsai is more important than another, the trunk's structure certainly is central to the tree's style. A thick trunk indicates a mature tree (whether or not it actually is old), but a too-thick trunk can make the tree look out of proportion. A good rule to guide you — but certainly not an absolute one — is that the height of the tree should be about six times the width of the trunk's base. The actual height depends on the style of the planting, the thickness of the tree, and the spread of the lowest branches.

Avoid trees with perfectly cylindrical trunks — those having the same thickness at the top as at the bottom. Trees with several curves in the trunk aren't as attractive as those with just one or two curves. In most cases, gentle bends or curves are more appealing than abrupt ones. A trunk should never curve toward the front.

The trunk should taper gracefully and naturally to its terminal point. The top of the tree should never be just lopped off to create an apex. If a tree is too tall, cut off the top portion with a taper cut (the cut surface should face the back of the tree). Or you can peel off the bark at the apex to create *jin* (see below).

If the apex is too low or is otherwise out of proportion to the rest of the tree, you can cut off the trunk just above a strong branch on the front side. Then create a new apex by wiring the strong branch upward to continue the trunk form with more suitable dimensions.

Highly desirable are trunks with aged, weather-beaten characteristics, but not trunks with such unsightly malformations as scars from incorrect wiring and pruning techniques. As you grow in skill,

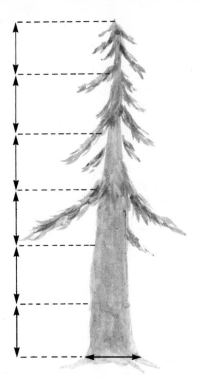

HEIGHT of bonsai should equal about six times the width of the trunk at its base.

you'll perfect techniques for creating the illusion of age.

By stripping off bark in the right places, for example, you can create *shari* and *jin* — areas of dead wood that are to a tree what a long gray beard is to a man. *Jin* is the dead tip of a trunk or branch; it is especially effective at the apex of a conifer. *Shari* is an area of dead wood on a living trunk or branch (see page 64 for details of these techniques).

(Continued on page 24)

SCARRED TRUNKS and branches appear naturally formed. Jin (at tip of trunk or branch) and shari (other dead areas) help create illusion of age.

23

Bonsai design

. . . Continued from page 23

Some bonsai enthusiasts use no tools to prune, choosing instead to twist or splinter branches off so they will appear broken by natural forces of wind or lightning. Done inexpertly, this kind of pruning can result in more harm than good. It's not a safe technique for the beginner.

<u>Branches.</u> These illustrate perfectly the fact that bonsai is not simply a miniature duplication of a tree in the wild. Left alone, trees often branch heavily and randomly. Most bonsai, in contrast, have relatively few branches, and those they have are carefully directed and spaced. The pattern of the branches establishes the basic outline of the tree and allows the trunk to be shown to its best advantage.

In the upright and slanting styles, the lowest branch should start about a third of the way up the trunk. This branch should be the largest one, extending out either to the left or to the right side and perhaps slightly toward the front. (With a slanting style or a curved trunk, this branch should go in the opposite direction of the slant or curve.)

Next, a somewhat smaller branch should extend in the opposite direction of the lowest branch and a little higher. Both should angle slightly toward the front of the tree. At a level between these two is a branch extending out toward the back.

This general pattern can be repeated to the top of the tree, the branches decreasing in size as they approach the top. Branches that extend directly out of the front of the tree are usually undesirable, especially low ones. Small, front-pointing branches in the upper third of the tree are called ornaments and can be kept on if they add to the design of the tree. Branches on opposite sides of the trunk should not be at the same level. A branch on the same side of the trunk should not be directly above a lower branch.

In the semicascade and cascade styles, the branches closest to the roots are the largest, with subsequent branches diminishing in size as they approach the tip. The apex is usually a large branch growing upward out of the back of the trunk just before the cascade turns downward.

Branches should vary in size and length, and spaces between branches should also vary, gradually diminishing toward the top. Having the bottom branch long, the next one shorter, and the next one still shorter may well create an effect that is much too stylized and stiff; an exception, though, is the formal upright style.

A rule of thumb is that the combined length of the two longest branches (usually the bottom two) equals about half the height of the tree. But you may have a rather short tree with an extremely thick trunk, and in this case the length of the two longest branches might total more than the height of the tree. The angle of slope should be roughly the same for all branches (remember that since the

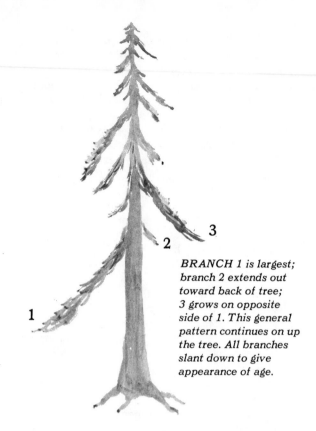

BRANCH 1 *is largest; branch 2 extends out toward back of tree; 3 grows on opposite side of 1. This general pattern continues on up the tree. All branches slant down to give appearance of age.*

LOWEST BRANCH *grows in opposite direction of curve on a curved trunk. Use this rule to create balance.*

Front

BRANCH *configuration as seen from above shows that no branches extend toward front.*

branches of conifers point up when young and down when old, you'll want to train the lower ones, in particular, downward).

The shape of the individual branches is important. The branches should appear narrow from the front and should taper toward the tip. Seen from the top, they should be wider near the trunk and taper to a point at the tip in a diamond, triangular, or arrowhead shape.

Branches should have a significantly smaller diameter than the trunk. Branches with too large a girth create a sense of disproportion and should be removed.

Look for these branch characteristics when you select a plant for bonsai material. If some of the less important branches don't conform to these guidelines, use your judgment in removing them. Other branch characteristics to avoid are tangled branches, branches that cross over in front of the trunk, parallel branches (remove one of a pair), branches with exaggerated bends in them, most front-growing branches (except the ornaments described earlier), and any branches thicker in the middle or end portions than they are near the trunk.

Foliage. The role of bonsai foliage is to reveal and complement the trunk and branch structures of the plant. Thick foliage all over a tree obscures the tree's structure. Too sparse foliage, on the other hand, indicates an unhealthy tree. Ideal foliage is small and compact and usually grows in dense clusters. Leaves should indicate vitality and health without hiding the tree.

You can control where the leaves grow. To some extent, you can control how large they grow (see page 64), but since your control over their size is greatly limited, it's always best to pick small-leafed trees to train as bonsai. The plants suggested on pages 33-36 have small foliage; some large-leafed types to avoid are listed on page 36.

You may be able to reduce the size of some leaves a bit, but you can't reduce the sizes of flowers and fruits at all. In the case of flowering and fruiting trees, the dwarf varieties are often more practical for bonsai, though it's extraordinarily appealing to see an 8-inch-high cherry tree loaded with regular-size cherries. Such a bonsai may never compete with a juniper or a Japanese maple for a beauty prize, but it more than succeeds in inspiring amazement and delight.

Roots. Even when a bonsai planting is not grown in the exposed-root style, the appearance of the roots that are exposed is very important. You should be able to see the crown of the tree, where the roots join the trunk, as well as the very tops of the large roots as they go out from the base and down into the soil.

A tree with many surface roots is one with a good root structure. The roots should spread out in all

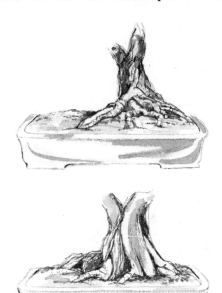

Good foliage

Too thick

FOLIAGE that is too thick obscures branch structure of a bonsai.

EXPOSED ROOTS at trunk's base add character.

Bonsai design

directions — not like spokes of a wheel, but with varying sizes and spacing. If there is an exceptionally large, protruding root, it should be at the back of the tree, never in the front.

Front and back. The thought of a tree in the forest having a front and a back seems rather odd. But a bonsai, of course, is a specially cultivated work of art, not a tree growing wild. For a bonsai, front and back are very important.

When you're preparing to train a plant, your first consideration is its front. That will be the side with the most potential for showing off the structure of the tree to best advantage. (When viewing a finished bonsai, if you're uncertain about which side is the front, look down on it from above to see in which direction the apex leans — it should lean toward the front.)

The front should be relatively open and airy, with no large branches protruding directly toward the viewer. Nor will a bonsai's front have a particularly large protruding section of root.

If you're starting with a seedling or a small nursery tree, you're unlikely to find one whose front side is perfect. Through pruning and wiring techniques, though, you will be able to correct most flaws. When deciding which is to be the front of the tree, give first consideration to the beauty of the plant — a subjective judgment best made only after careful study of the tree, other bonsai, and trees growing in the wild.

Often the esthetic consideration merges with the practical. Seen from one side, a given tree may have too many front-growing branches, a strongly front-curving trunk, or other defects. These you may not want to correct, or perhaps to correct them might create scars or other flaws. In this case you can choose another side for the front, not only on the basis of beauty but also with an eye to making your work with the plant easier.

The back of the tree is important not so much for itself as for what it adds to the appearance of the tree when seen from the front. Front-growing branches are often undesirable, but rear-growing ones are essential. These branches create a feeling of substance and depth. Bonsai should not be only two-dimensional — they need a vigorous, three-dimensional quality. Back branches help establish that quality and provide a good-looking backdrop of foliage.

Though the back is not viewed directly, it should be well tended. There should be no awkwardly shaped branches, no overpowering branches, no complexity of branch or foliage to take attention away from the front.

FRONT of tree has open feeling; no branches extend toward viewer.

BACK of tree has more branches to create feeling of depth.

TOP view shows good placement of branches. Apex leans toward front.

Compact clusters of foliage
show off structure of
branches to best advantage.

LODGEPOLE PINE. Pinus contorta
murrayana. *Height: 26 inches. Found growing
wild. Trained 7 years.*

JAPANESE BOXWOOD. Buxus
microphylla japonica. *Height: 11 inches.
Dug from a garden hedge 6 years ago
(hedge was 28 years old).*

CALIFORNIA SCRUB OAK. Quercus
dumosa. *Height: 22 inches. Found growing
wild. Trained 12 years.*

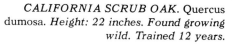

OLIVE. Olea europaea. *Height: 19 inches.*
Dug 31 years ago from a garden.

HOLLY OAK (Holm oak).
Quercus ilex. *Height: 20 inches.*
From seed. 31 years old.

 The trunk gives a tree its character; it is the soul of the bonsai.

BUTTONWOOD. Conocarpus erecta. *Height: 13 inches. Found growing wild. Trained 3 years.*

29

A glimpse of a tree's
roots reveals its bond
with the earth.

UTAH JUNIPER. Juniperus utahensis. *Height: 29
inches. Found growing wild. Trained 4 years.*

HORNBEAM. Carpinus. *Height: 21 inches. Imported from
Japan. 35 years old.*

JAPANESE WHITE PINE. Pinus parviflora.
Height: 16 inches. From seed. 10 years old.

Containers. As important as any element of the tree itself, the container you choose for your bonsai must be a harmonious part of the whole planting. In a sense, the right pot disappears — that is, it's not especially noticed when you are viewing the tree.

Earlier in bonsai history, the small plant was little more than an excuse to show off the potter's finest work. Beautiful pots, gorgeously glazed, were the rule. Today, glazed pots are most often used with fruiting, flowering, and other deciduous trees. Evergreen trees look best with unglazed containers in such dark colors as brown, red brown, gray, and dull purple. With deciduous trees you can use glazed pots, but don't overpower the tree with the pot. Select darker shades for plants with dark, rich foliage, lighter shades for plants with light foliage.

Shape and size of the pot are important, too. Again, the principle is to harmonize with the whole. For cascade-style bonsai, use round or equilateral pots that are several inches deep in order to maintain a sense of balance with the tree. For upright and group styles, use round, rectangular, or oval pots.

The depth of the pot is usually the same as the thickness of the trunk's base (in a group planting, the base of the thickest trunk). The length of a pot for a single upright tree should be about ⅔ the height of the tree. The length of a pot for a group planting should be about ⅓ the height of the tallest tree. For the multiple-trunk style, the length of the pot should be about ⅔ the height of the tallest trunk.

In general, all shallow pots present a straight side to the front. Deep pots may present either a straight side or a corner to the front. A deep hexagonal pot always has a corner to the front.

To get a feeling for which pots look best with which trees, look at the bonsai pictured in this book and cast a discerning eye on those you see at exhibits. In choosing the right pot for a tree, just as in the other decisions you will make in training your bonsai, it's your esthetic judgment you have to depend on. That judgment will make the tree uniquely yours.

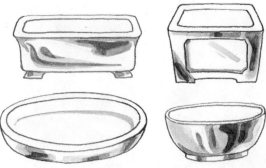

PLANT UPRIGHT and group styles in rectangular or oval pot with main trunk slightly off-center.

PLANT CASCADE or slanting styles in center of round or equilateral container.

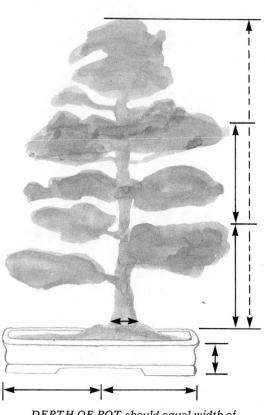

DEPTH OF POT should equal width of trunk at its base (above). Length should approximate two-thirds the height of the tree or, in a multiple-trunk style (right), height of tallest trunk.

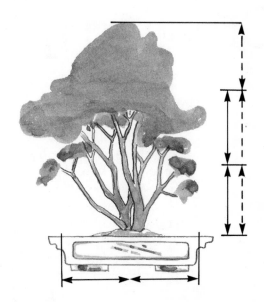

Bonsai design

EXPERT ponders whether to add azalea to rock planting. See results on page 58.

Creating Your Own Bonsai

What do you want in a bonsai? A classic evergreen, like a pine? A deciduous tree that will take you through the seasons — a maple, for example?

Look at the pictures of bonsai in this book, in exhibits, anywhere you can find them. Decide what kind of plant appeals to you, what you would like to try. If a particular style intrigues you, such as a cascade or a forest planting, check pages 34-36 for the kinds of trees that do best in that style.

Once you know what kind of tree you want to work with, let this section guide you in learning how to acquire the tree, plant it, train it, care for it, and display it.

These plants make good bonsai

If you're just beginning, you'll probably find it easier to work with the more common bonsai plants. Most of those listed below are readily available at nurseries and are hardy enough that they won't simply keel over and die if you make a few mistakes as you're learning.

As your skill in working with bonsai grows, you'll want to be more adventurous, try more unusual plants. Though some plants take to container growing better than others, almost any kind of woody plant material is worth a try. You just might make a bonsai of a plant that no one has been successful with before.

Look for trees with small leaves, fruits, and flowers. Leaf size can be reduced somewhat (see page 64), but fruit and flower size can't be changed. A dwarf variety used as bonsai will seldom match the look or the vigor of a full-grown tree in the wild. Dwarf varieties that do work well are included in the lists below.

Plants listed under "Some that don't work" are there for any of several reasons. Some are just too large; others grow too vigorously or don't like having their roots confined.

The lists suggesting particular plants for particular styles are guidelines only. The final decision depends on the tree and on your judgment.

Old favorites

Ezo spruce (*Picea jezoensis*)

Flowering cherry (*Prunus subhirtella, P. yedoensis*)

Hinoki false cypress (*Chamaecyparis obtusa*)

Kurume azalea (*Rhododendron* Kurume hybrids)

Maidenhair tree (*Ginkgo biloba*)

Maples: Japanese maple (*Acer palmatum*), Trident maple (*A. buergerianum*)

Pines: Japanese black pine (*Pinus thunbergiana*), Mugho pine (*P. mugo mughus*)

Sawleaf zelkova (*Zelkova serrata*)

Shimpaku, Sargent juniper (*Juniperus chinensis sargentii*)

Wisteria: Japanese wisteria (*Wisteria floribunda*), Chinese wisteria (*W. sinensis*)

Japanese black pine

Choosing a plant

Good choices for the beginner

Cotoneaster (*Cotoneaster conspicua* 'Decora', *C. dammeri, C. microphylla*)

Dwarf hemlock (*Tsuga sieboldii* 'Nana')

Dwarf pomegranate (*Punica granatum* 'Nana')

Juniper (*Juniperus scopulorum, J. virginiana*)

Pyracantha or Firethorn (*Pyracantha species*)

Pyracantha (Firethorn)

Consider these for group plantings

Beech (*Fagus crenata, F. sieboldii, F. sylvatica*)

Chinese elm (*Ulmus parvifolia*)

Deodar cedar (*Cedrus deodara*)

European white birch (*Betula verrucosa;* also sold as *B. alba* or *B. pendula*)

Fir (*Abies* species)

Hemlock (*Tsuga* species)

Maidenhair tree (*Ginkgo biloba*)

Maples: Japanese maple (*Acer palmatum*), Trident maple (*A. buergerianum*)

Oak (*Quercus dentata, Q. serrata*)

Sawleaf zelkova (*Zelkova serrata*)

Sweet gum (*Liquidambar* species)

Japanese maple

These cascade

Atlas cedar (*Cedrus atlantica*)

Azalea (*Rhododendron* species)

Cascade chrysanthemum (*Chrysanthemum morifolium*)

Cotoneaster (*Cotoneaster rotundifolia, C. horizontalis*)

English hawthorn (*Crataegus oxyacantha*)

Fig (*Ficus carica*)

Honeysuckle (*Lonicera japonica*)

Japanese black pine (*Pinus thunbergiana*)

Japanese maple (*Acer palmatum*)

Japanese wisteria (*Wisteria floribunda*)

Pyracantha or Firethorn (*Pyracantha species*)

Shimpaku or Sargent juniper (*Juniperus chinensis sargentii*)

Shimpaku (Sargent juniper)

Azalea (*Rhododendron* species)

Beech (*Fagus crenata, F. sieboldii, F. sylvatica*)

Dogwood (*Cornus controversa, C. kousa*)

English ivy (*Hedera helix*)

European white birch (*Betula verrucosa, B. alba,* or *B. pendula*)

Fig (*Ficus carica*)

Japanese holly (*Ilex crenata*)

Japanese maple (*Acer palmatum*)

Maidenhair tree (*Ginkgo biloba*)

Mugho pine (*Pinus mugo mughus*)

Oak (*Quercus dentata, Q. serrata*)

Olive (*Olea europaea*)

Pomegranate (*Punica granatum*)

Pyracantha or Firethorn (*Pyracantha species*)

Shimpaku or Sargent juniper (*Juniperus chinensis sargentii*)

These often have multiple trunks

Mugho pine

Choosing a plant

Plant these on a rock

Chinese elm (*Ulmus parvifolia*)

Cypress (*Taxodium distichum*)

Ezo spruce (*Picea jezoensis*)

Pines: Dwarf stone pine (*Pinus pumila*), Japanese black pine (*P. thunbergiana*), Japanese white pine (*P. parviflora*), Japanese red pine (*P. densiflora*)

Rock cotoneaster (*Cotoneaster horizontalis*)

Shimpaku or Sargent juniper (*Juniperus chinensis sargentii*)

Trident maple (*Acer buergerianum*)

Shimpaku (Sargent juniper)

Try one in a slanted style

Azalea (*Rhododendron* species)

Beech (*Fagus crenata, F. sieboldii, F. sylvatica*)

English hawthorn (*Crataegus oxyacantha*)

European white birch (*Betula verrucosa, B. alba,* or *B. pendula*)

Ezo spruce (*Picea jezoensis*)

Japanese larch (*Larix leptolepis*)

Japanese maple (*Acer palmatum*)

Oak (*Quercus dentata, Q. serrata*)

Olive (*Olea europaea*)

Pines (*Pinus species*)

Pomegranate (*Punica granatum*)

Shimpaku or Sargent juniper (*Juniperus chinensis sargentii*)

Star jasmine (*Trachelospermum jasminoides*)

Japanese black pine

Some that don't work

American mountain ash (*Sorbus americana*)

Chinese pistache (*Pistacia chinensis*)

Eucalyptus

Longleaf pine (*Pinus palustris*)

Madrone (*Arbutus menziesii*)

Manzanita (*Arctostaphylos* species)

Mountain mahogany (*Cercocarpus betuloides*)

Rangpur lime (*Citrus aurantifolia* 'Rangpur')

Southern magnolia (*Magnolia grandiflora*)

Weeping willow (*Salix babylonica*)

Western red cedar (*Thuja plicata*)

Getting started

The traditional way of starting a bonsai is to collect a plant growing wild, pot it, and wait several years before training it. This technique is described on pages 48-50. Because this method robs the environment of trees, though, and because there's such a long wait before training can even begin, the other methods described in this section have become accepted as equally valid ways of starting bonsai. One of the best ways to be assured of success — and therefore one of the best ways for the beginner — is to start with a nursery plant. The plant lists on the previous pages can help you find the right one.

From the nursery

Nurseries have a wide variety of potential bonsai plants, and nursery personnel can give you advice about a plant's growth habits. Having grown up in containers of 5-gallon size or less, the root systems of nursery plants have adapted to confined conditions, and transplanting them will prove much less traumatic than with plants dug out of the ground.

The artful shopper

When you shop for your potential bonsai, know the characteristics you want. Look for a vigorous, healthy tree with small, compact foliage. Try to find one that's not too tall and gawky and one that has a thick, strong trunk at the base (dig down to see if some of the trunk is under the soil surface). Look carefully at the shape and arrangement of major branches — you might have to push some foliage gently aside to do this. Try to imagine which side would be the front, which the back (see page 26 for a discussion of front and back).

Ask yourself some questions. Would any major branches have to be removed? If so, would the pruning leave visible scars? Let the tree suggest the basic form — upright, slanting, and so forth. Then imagine how you want the finished planting to look. What will you need to do to accomplish that — bend the trunk, wire the branches, create a new apex?

The castoff plant that doesn't get a second look from other gardeners may be exactly the right specimen for your bonsai. It's the one with the bent or twisted trunk, the dwarfish character, that the bonsai grower rescues from ignominy and turns into a work of art.

Out of a nursery can

After you've chosen your tree, have the can cut only if you expect to repot the plant as soon as you get home. When a can is cut, roots dry out fast.

Trim back the root ball by about a third and put the tree into a container that is slightly smaller than the one you took it from. Try to flatten out the ball shape somewhat. Don't expect to chop away enormous amounts of roots all at one time to get a canned tree into a small bonsai container. Few plants will survive this treatment.

At the next replanting season (see Seasonal Care Chart, pages 76-77) thin the roots even more and transfer the tree to its shallow bonsai container. By working in this gradual way, you'll be able to get the root system down to the right size without danger of losing the plant (see pages 51-55 for details on planting).

Working with a balled tree

If you come across a balled tree even 3 or 4 feet tall and see it as a potential bonsai, buy it — it may not be there next time.

When you get it home don't cut it down to size all at once. Pot it in a big container, one large enough that the root ball won't be disturbed. Plant the entire root ball; the burlap will rot. Be sure to leave about 1½ inches between the top of the soil and the edge of the container for watering. Cut off the top third of the tree, prune the branches to shape, and wire, if desired.

Leave the giant bonsai in the container for 2 years, continuing to prune and shape it. Then transplant it to a smaller container, cutting back the roots to fit. Shape for another year, then go to a smaller container, and so on until the tree is the size you want.

Peat pot beginnings

A well-watered plant in a peat pot will have small roots growing out of the sides and bottom. In this case you can plant pot and all right in the bonsai container, breaking away about an inch of the pot's rim; the rest of the peat will gradually dissolve into the soil. The tree will suffer little or no setback from transplanting.

If the peat pot is bone dry, with no roots growing through the sides or bottom, it needs special handling. Here, it's best to crack the pot and carefully peel it away. After gently separating the roots, plant only the root ball.

Bonsai from seed

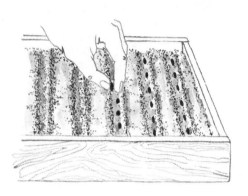

1. *IN A FLAT, plant seeds in rows. Cover surface with damp moss.*

2. *OR PLANT seeds in pots — a few in each. Keep soil warm and moist.*

3. *SEEDLINGS are ready to transplant when two sets of leaves appear.*

4. *YOUNG PLANT must mature 2 years before it's ready for bonsai pot.*

To the avid gardener, few things are more satisfying than starting a plant from the very beginning — not with seedlings, cuttings, or young nursery trees, but with seed.

The drawback, though, is time — the radish and the tree inhabit the same kingdom, but the radish sprints from seed to finish, while the tree is a long-distance runner. In other words, if you start your bonsai from seed, you will have to wait much longer than if you propagate in other ways. Still, if you're patient enough, your reward will be almost complete control over the shape of your plant from the beginning, and drastic pruning will probably never be necessary.

Some plants to try from seed are maple, beech, pomegranate, ginkgo, zelkova, tupelo (sourgum), liquidambar (sweet gum), larch, buckeye, sweet chestnut, spruce, pine, oak, and hornbeam. You can buy seed from nurseries or mail-order seed companies — ask at your nursery which companies specialize in bonsai seeds. Or you can gather seeds in the wild. In any case, get more seed than you need, since not all of them will germinate.

The best time to sow seeds for bonsai is early spring, and doing this will require some advance planning. In order to sprout most alpine and Japanese species (pine, spruce), place the seeds in a plastic bag containing a mixture of one part sand and one part peat moss, and put seeds, bag, and all in the refrigerator at 34°-40°. The length of their stay will vary, depending on the kind of plant; ask your seed supplier for specific information (60 to 90 days is a general guideline).

If you can't find out the length of time to keep your seeds refrigerated, check them daily and plant them at the first sign of sprouting. Sow the seeds in the half sand, half peat mixture.

Low elevation natives (buckeye, oak, apricot, pecan, dwarf pomegranate) don't usually need to be refrigerated. They should be kept dry until they're sown in the very early spring.

To water, place the seed container in water and let the water soak upward to the surface of the soil. This method eliminates any chance of washing away the soil that covers the seed. You can water the soil surface with a fine spray if you are careful not to disturb the topsoil. Covering the surface with damp sphagnum moss will help the soil retain moisture until the seeds germinate.

Keep the container outdoors or in a coldframe (see page 73), situated to avoid strong, direct afternoon sun that would dry out the soil too much and too fast. The soil temperature should remain between 65° and 75° for germination.

It shouldn't take much more than a week or two for the seeds to germinate. Once they've germinated, remove any moss covering, put the container

where it can get abundant sunlight, and water and weed the new plants regularly.

When two sets of leaves appear, lift out the hardiest plants and transplant them into light, sandy soil in 2-inch pots. Shorten the roots so they don't curl at the bottom of the pot.

Reexamine the roots in early summer. If they're beginning to curl, cut them again so they are straight. At this time, you can replant the seedling into a 4-inch pot or into open ground.

Seedlings transplanted into the ground should be placed about 2 feet apart to allow plenty of room for root development. Dig the plants up every year, prune their roots back by ⅓, and plant them in a new location.

Whether you plant the seedling in the ground or in a container, you can begin to control its basic shape somewhat by pinching back new growth (see page 63) as it appears. Not until 2 years have passed will the plant be ready to be moved into its bonsai pot to begin more intensive training.

Cuttings are easy

Taking cuttings — a long-time favorite propagating technique of house plant gardeners — works as well for almost all bonsai plants, with the exception of pines. Olive, willow, cotoneaster, pyracantha, azalea, rhododendron, spruce, juniper, maple, and boxwood are especially easy to propagate this way, and starting a bonsai from a cutting is much faster than starting one from seed.

The best time to take cuttings is in early spring, just before brand-new buds open, or in autumn,

before the parent plant becomes fully dormant. Since a cutting is a section of a larger plant, you can be sure that it will mimic the form and quality of its parent.

The best cuttings are made from the nonflowering side shoots of vigorous, healthy plants. If the stem snaps when you bend it, it's ready for cutting. If it bends or crushes, it's either too young or too old.

← Make second cut here

← Cut branch here first

1. Take several more cuttings than you will need, since — like seeds — not all of them will take. Make them 2 to 5 inches long, being certain that they have at least three buds.

Cut across the branch just above a bud, as shown. Remove all leaves and any buds in the bottom ½ inch of the stem, but retain the top leaves. They'll provide food for the cutting until roots have formed.

Now cut the stem as shown at a 45° angle just below the bottom node. It's from this node that the new roots will grow.

(Continued on next page)

Getting started

... Continued from page 39

2. Certain types of conifers and some semi-hardwood plants (arborvitae, azalea, cotone-aster, daphne, jasmine, lilac, myrtle, pyracantha, weigela, and yew, for example) do better if they're rooted from cuttings with what's called a "heel." This means that when you take the cutting, you'll also include a small portion of the older or larger branch. Remove a heel cutting from the parent plant with a very sharp knife, being careful not to rip the bark and leave a ragged cut. Trim the heel so that the edges and the surface of the cut are smooth.

3. If you have some cuttings with particularly thick stems, you'll want to taper or notch them as shown in order to promote new root growth.

4. Though you can root species in water, it's safer to use sand or a sandy soil mixture. (See page 52 for a basic soil mix you can use.) Fill a flat or 3-inch-deep box with the soil to within about ½ inch of the top. First soak the soil; then make rows 2 inches apart and about an inch deep.

    Dip the end of each cutting into some water, then into a hormone-fungicide powder, following the directions on the package label. Next, set the cuttings into the sand or soil mixture, burying at least two nodes below the surface. Carefully firm the soil around the cuttings so they'll stand upright. Keep the soil moist, but don't allow it to get waterlogged or the cuttings will rot. Keep them out of direct sunlight and mist the leaves regularly.

Nodes go below soil level

5. Clear plastic bags or glass jars can be placed down over the cuttings to create tiny individual greenhouses that help retain the soil's moisture.

Conifers need an extra push before being planted — put the cuttings in water for several hours first, with the bottom of the stem submerged and the foliage out of the water.

Depending on the kind of plant, the cuttings should be well established in 6 months to a year. To be certain, keep them in the rooting medium for a full year or until vigorous new growth appears. After that, treat them the same as seedlings (see page 39). You can transplant them into pots or plant them directly in the ground, taking care to protect them from extremes of sunlight and wind until they've taken hold in their new environment.

Grafting is tricky

Grafting takes a good bit of skill, but it is the only way to unite two plants with complementary characteristics. For example, you can join a fast grower with one that has good, compact foliage. The major drawback to grafting bonsai is that even after a graft has taken successfully, a scar remains. Plants that can be successfully grafted are wisteria, ginkgo, pomegranate, flowering apricot, plum, peach, pear, persimmon, crabapple, cherry, and maple.

In grafting, the rooted plant that receives the graft is called the "stock"; the branch that is grafted onto the rooted stock is called the "scion." Grafting scions should be taken from trees whose leaves

are good for bonsai (small leaves in compact, dense clusters are ideal) but whose growth is slow. They should be grafted to trees of the same genus which are fast growing. Probably the most common bonsai graft unites a Japanese white pine (*Pinus parviflora*) with a Japanese black pine (*Pinus thunbergiana*). The black pine is a faster grower than the white pine; the white has smaller needles.

Grafting is usually done in early spring when the buds are dormant and just as the sap is beginning to flow; it can also be done in winter.

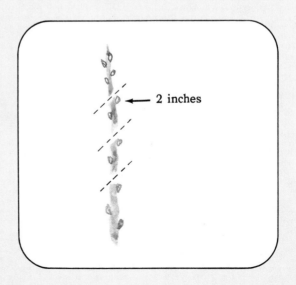

← 2 inches

Scions should be cut from a parent plant shoot 36 inches long or less. Make the cutting the previous fall (after the plant is fully dormant) and keep it buried in the ground about ⅔ of its length or wrapped in plastic and refrigerated. Two inches is maximum length for scions, and each should have 2 to 4 buds. The stock should be a healthy seedling no more than 3 years old. You can graft scions onto the top of the stock or onto the side.

Top grafting

Two kinds of top grafting are fairly simple to do — cleft grafting and whip grafting. The stock should be about ½ inch in diameter where the graft is to be made.

Cleft grafting is done this way:

1. Cut the stock straight across, leaving a few groups of leaves or needles on the stem.

2. Lay a grafting tool or a very sharp knife across the end of the cut and tap it in with a small hammer to make a cleft about ½ inch deep through bark and all.

3. The scion should be the same diameter as the stock. Cut its lower end into a wedge shape and insert it into the split stock, making certain the cambium layers of the two pieces match. (Cambium is the soft layer of tissue between the bark and the wood.) Leave just a little of the cut surface of the scion exposed above the surface of the stock, since this makes for a stronger union. If the scion is not as thick as the stock, place it off-center so that one outer edge is flush with the outer edge of the stock.

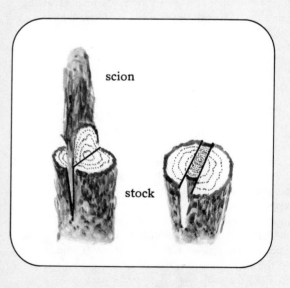

scion

stock

4. Bind the graft with raffia or grafting rubber bands as shown and then cover it all over with grafting wax.

Keep grafted plants outdoors, but protect them from wind and direct sunlight and water them generously for about 2 weeks. After that they can receive direct sun and fewer, though regular, waterings.

By the next growing season the scion should show some new growth. If not, it hasn't taken and you'll have to try again the following season with new cuttings.

Whip grafting allows you to graft small scions on small stocks. It's a handy method for adding a branch to a tree where an unsightly gap can't be filled in by another branch wired or tied into place.

Make a slanting cut through both the stock and the scion as shown. Then make a second cut into each piece, starting about ⅓ of the distance from opposite tips, cutting almost parallel to the original cut. Fit the scion and the stock together, wrap the union with raffia, and cover the whole thing with grafting wax. Aftercare is the same as for cleft grafts.

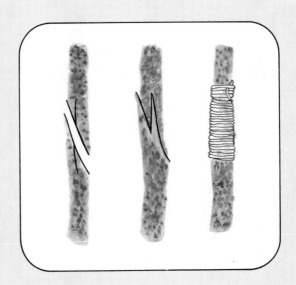

Side grafting

Use side grafting with heavier stock — thicker than ½ inch. Begin by preparing the scion. Cut it in a wedge shape, but give the wedge unequal sides. The inner side should be longer than the outer side. Next, make a cut in the side of the stock where the scion is to fit. Insert the scion (shorter cut down), wrap the graft with raffia, and cover the entire union with grafting wax. Trim the stock back to just a few leaves. Aftercare is the same as for other grafts.

Getting started

Create a whole tree by layering

Layering is a simple, convenient, and rather fascinating way of increasing a plant by rooting branches while they're still attached to the parent plant. The layered plant has the same advantage a seedling has — no large taproot to contend with — and the added advantage of having a woody trunk structure already well on its way to maturity.

It's not unusual to find a branch of a tree that's a natural sport (mutation), that has smaller leaves than the other branches, or that has a particularly fine shape. Layering lets you make this branch into your bonsai.

Plants that particularly lend themselves to this kind of propagation (best carried out in early spring) include maple, azalea, crape myrtle, willow, camellia, cryptomeria, Sargent juniper, pomegranate, elm, wisteria, zelkova, flowering quince, forsythia, and Ezo spruce.

The minute it is detached from its parent, the layered branch is well on its way to being a good bonsai specimen and can be planted in its own bonsai pot or in the ground. Use earth layering with a branch growing close to the ground, air layering with a branch higher up.

Air layering

There are three ways to go about air layering. This is the most reliable method:

1. Wrap copper wire like a tourniquet once around the branch about an inch below the place where you want the roots to grow.

2. Next, using sphagnum moss that has been soaked in water, pack moist moss tightly around the new-root area in a ball shape. The diameter of the ball of sphagnum should be at least three or four times the diameter of the branch.

3. Wrap the moss ball with agricultural plastic and tie it with string at top and bottom. The plastic will allow you to observe the growth of the new roots and will also keep the moss from drying out.

Trees that grow roots very fast, such as those mentioned on the opposite page, will be ready for removal from the parent plant in 3 to 6 months. Pines, on the other hand, won't form a root system for 1, 2, or even 3 years.

Two air layering variations work faster than the tourniquet method and are more commonly used but not as reliable. One calls for making a cut into the branch; the other requires that a ring of bark be peeled from the branch. Once in awhile, though, these methods cause a branch to die.

The illustrations below show how to air layer by making a cut in the branch and by peeling off a ring of bark. Make the cut about ⅓ the diameter of the branch, just below where the new roots are to grow. If you're peeling bark, remove a ring of bark about ¾ inch wide around the branch.

Dust the cut or peeled area with hormone powder to give it added resistance to disease. Coat it with moist clay.

To keep the cut branch from growing back together, insert a pebble into the cut, wedging it open. Wrap the cut or peeled area in a large ball of wet sphagnum moss and hold it all together with agricultural plastic, as shown at left and above for the tourniquet method.

Before you plant an air layered specimen, remove all the sphagnum from around the new roots that have formed. Because roots will be fine and very delicate, be extremely careful when you're removing the moss. Broken or torn roots greatly diminish your new tree's chances for survival. As you lift off the pieces of moss, look for the fragile little root hairs. Some experts use tweezers to pull off very small amounts of the moss at a time.

CUT branch ⅓ its diameter.   *PEBBLE in cut keeps it open.*   *OR PEEL off ring of bark.*

Getting started

Earth layering

If you discover a suitable branch growing close to the ground, try earth layering. The principle is the same as in air layering — the forcing of new root growth by branch injury. But in this method the growth medium for new roots is not a ball of wet moss but the ground itself.

1. Check the branch to see whether it can be bent down to the ground. If you can bend it far enough without snapping it, make a cut on its underside where you want the new roots to grow. Cut to a depth equal to roughly ⅓ of the branch's diameter. Coat the cut area with hormone powder and moist clay. Insert a small pebble into the cut to keep it from growing back together.

2. If the branch is supple enough, you can bury the layered part entirely underground, packing the soil firmly around it to hold the branch in place. If it's less supple, bring it down to the ground, stake it in place as shown, and build up a mound of soil around it. In either case, for a well-draining growing medium, mix the ground soil you use with equal parts of peat moss, ground bark, and sand.

3. Softwood plants, such as serissa, weigela, parthenocissus, forsythia, will root very fast, some as soon as 6 to 8 weeks. With rhododendron, azalea, and other hardwood shrubs, it's best to layer old branches. If the layered area is kept moist, hardwood shrubs should develop new roots in about a year. (You can *very carefully* remove some of the earth from time to time to check on the progress of the new root system.) Once several roots have developed, you can sever the new tree from the parent and plant it in its own pot or in the open ground.

Two plants from one

Dividing is the gardener's own two-for-one sale. You take a plant out of a nursery can or out of the ground, divide the root mass and the above-ground parts into sections, and presto — where you once had a single plant, you now have two or more, ready to be planted separately.

Shrubs and perennials with multiple trunks (such as hydrangea, wisteria, cotoneaster, flowering cherry, rhododendron, bamboo, pomegranate, daphne, and chrysanthemum) can be divided quickly and easily. Early spring, just before new growth appears, is the best time for dividing plants.

1. Dig out the root mass with a spading fork and separate it into sections. Sometimes you'll need to cut the roots apart with a sharp knife.

2. You can divide pomegranate and chrysanthemum by cutting new shoots off the roots as shown and planting the shoots separately. The shoots should be about 3 inches long.

3. To divide bamboo and wisteria, simply cut off a 2-inch section of a mature root or rhizome (underground stem) and plant it separately. These sections should sprout the following spring.

(Continued on next page)

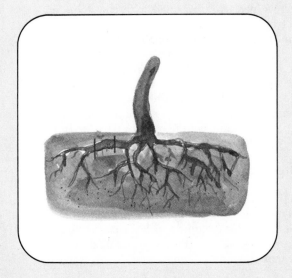

Getting started

... *Continued from page 47*

Dust the roots with hormone powder to prevent rot, and then set the newly divided plants in individual pots with fresh soil or in freshly prepared beds in the ground.

Though a divided plant should be a healthy adult, the dividing is a shock to its system and it will need time to recuperate. Don't begin training until new roots are firmly established — normally, they'll be going strong in about 6 months.

Gathering trees in the wild

Most bonsai of great age have spent most of their lives in natural surroundings, growing in the earth or in cracks in rocks. During their years in the wild they were exposed to all manner of climatic extremes, physical abuses, and deprivations. Many of them have gone through tremendous struggles to survive.

Traditionally, such plants make the very best bonsai. They have developed a form that speaks of their environment; they look old, often older than they actually are; they have become adapted to existing under adverse conditions. When such plants are put into containers, they invariably outshine most if not all other specimens that may be displayed around them. And gathering trees from the wild, of course, is how it all began. In Japan the hunt for natural dwarfs has gone on for centuries, making it rare to find good specimens outside protected areas.

Because bonsai is still quite new here in the United States, our wilderness has not been stripped of naturally dwarfed trees. But the ever-increasing popularity of bonsai should give nature lovers cause to consider the botanical repercussions of an onslaught of dwarf-hungry tree gatherers in our delicately balanced wild places.

If you do gather in the wild, be very selective about the trees you dig up. Study all the possibilities so you're not halfway through digging up one tree when another one catches your eye. Remember, you're especially concerned with the shape of the trunk; it's old wood and you won't be able to train it into a different configuration. When digging up the tree, disturb as little of the surrounding flora as possible. Be certain to abide by all local regulations regarding the removing of natural objects. Most if not all public parks, for instance, prohibit the removal of any flora. If you're going onto private land, get the owner's permission before removing any plant life.

When to gather

The best season for gathering trees for bonsai is early spring — *before new buds open.* Plants would experience the greatest shock right after new buds opened. Before they open, though, plants will undergo a minimum of shock from being uprooted and transplanted into a new environment. It is possible to do a successful transplanting in seasons other than early spring, but the chances for success are much slimmer.

If you want to try transplanting deciduous trees in summer, remove about half the tree's leaves from the branches at the time of digging. This greatly reduces the amount of energy the plant has to use supplying nourishment to the leaves — energy it needs to adapt to the new environment. It also greatly reduces transpiration (loss of water), which you can further reduce by spraying the foilage with an antitranspirant spray (available at nurseries). There is a period of time in early fall, after summer-long growth has finished and before twigs harden, when you might try transplanting pines and other conifers.

In the winter months most plants are dormant. Transplanting during this period means disturbing root systems that won't be able to muster up enough energy to reestablish themselves.

It's certainly best to collect only in early spring, unless at another time of year you happen across a plant in the wild that you just can't do without. If there's little likelihood of losing the plant to another collector, wait till spring.

What to take on a collecting trip

The tree gatherer, like the back packer, likes to travel as lightly as possible. A shovel's not enough, but neither do you need a portable greenhouse on your back. Here is a list of necessary tools:

- Small shovel. The collapsible army type is good. You'll have to dig more than you would with a big one, but it's lightweight and has a sharp end.
- Sharp shears. You'll probably need these for cutting fairly thick roots.
- Sphagnum moss. Moistened and wrapped around roots, it helps keep plants alive.
- Container of water. The water is necessary for keeping leaves and roots wet on the trip home.
- Small pry bar. Some trees may be wedged tightly into cracks in rocks. You'll need to pry them out.
- Burlap or polyethylene sheeting and stout string or balling nails. Wrap root balls in the burlap sheeting; secure the wrapping with string or nails.

Out of the ground...to a new home

Take a substantial amount of the surrounding soil with the tree to protect the roots. Start by clearing away all ground growth from around the base of the trunk. Next, prune away all unnecessary branches. On the ground, draw a circle around the tree. The circle's diameter should be the equivalent of at least ⅓ the height of the tree. Larger-spreading trees require larger circles — their root spread duplicates the spread of the branches.

Start digging downward, following the circle's circumference. Use your shears to cut any tough roots (always cut roots on the diagonal). Keep digging until the depth of the trench you've made is about the same as the diameter of the circle. At this point start digging under the tree from all sides in toward the center. If it's at all possible, avoid cutting the taproot. If the taproot goes too deep you'll have to cut it, but do it as low as possible.

Once you've dug completely around and under the root ball, work the plant very gently back and forth, easing it out of the hole. Wrap the root ball completely with well-soaked sphagnum moss. Don't leave any part unprotected. Cover the whole thing with polyethylene sheeting and tie it up.

Once the plant is out of the ground, it's very important to treat it gently and carefully. Certain precautions are essential when you're transporting it home. Secure it so it can't roll about and damage its branches. Make sure the foliage has good air circulation (don't put it in the trunk of the car) and is protected from direct wind and sunlight. It's crucial that the foliage have plenty of moisture.

Keep it damp with a sprayer — you'll probably have to spray several times.

Plant the tree the minute you arrive home. You can plant it directly in the ground or in a large tub or planter box. If it has many delicate roots close to the base, you can plant it in a deep pot along with all the soil that came with it. (It's easy to tell if it has fine roots — they will keep the soil around the root ball from dropping away.)

If, instead, the plant has only a few large roots, it's better to plant it in the ground first, to be transferred to a training pot later. The soil in your garden should be fine for it — unless it's been heavily fertilized recently. Your tree won't be strong enough to have a first feeding for a few months. Dig a hole in the ground large enough to accommodate the roots, and plant the tree along with the soil that remained with the root ball.

When the tree has been planted, either in a pot or in the ground, trim off any roots poking above the surface. Continue to protect the plant from wind and direct sunlight. Water moderately and moisten the foliage often; in very warm weather you should spray the foliage several times a day.

In just a few months, new roots will form. At this time the plant should be hardy enough to look the sun straight in the eye without protection. About the same time, it's ready for its first feeding. (For fertilizing details, see page 73.) Keep the soil well-watered, but you can taper off on spraying the foliage — once a day at most is fine.

Other than daily care, don't disturb your new prize for a year, however much your green thumb may itch. At the end of that year you can remove

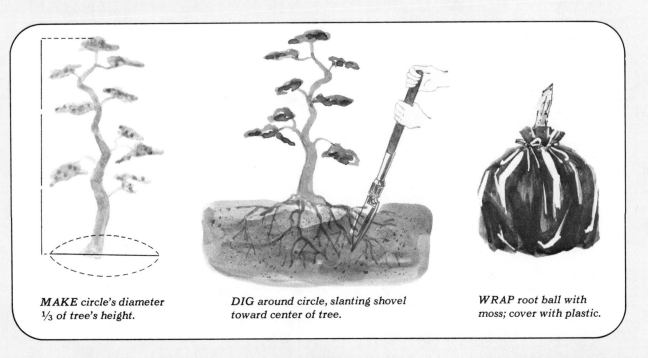

MAKE circle's diameter ⅓ of tree's height.

DIG around circle, slanting shovel toward center of tree.

WRAP root ball with moss; cover with plastic.

Getting started

the tree from the ground or from its pot for placement in a more shallow pot, but still not its bonsai container. Trim the remaining taproot back by ½ or more. If there are a large number of brand-new roots — the fine, hairy ones are the new roots — trim them back by about ⅓. If there aren't many new roots, just do a light pruning.

It's a good idea to do some branch pruning at this time too — there'll be less plant for the reduced rootage to supply with nourishment. Don't do any drastic pruning, but cut back young growth that isn't essential to the tree's basic shape (see page 62.) Once the roots have been pruned, place the plant in a pot with as much original soil on the root ball as possible. Fill in with new soil (see page 52 for a soil mix to use).

Even now you're not going to be able to do more with your tree than day-to-day care. After another year, remove it from its pot again, trim off the rest of the taproot, trim back new-root growth by ⅓, and put it into its shallow bonsai pot. (For further instructions on repotting, see page 74.) Now, 2 years after you collected it, it's ready for training.

For the beginner who wants to get on with it, collecting wild trees just isn't the way. Two years is a long, slow countdown. But once you're a confirmed bonsai enthusiast, you'll find a special satisfaction in working with a tree you came upon on a mountain hike, removed gently from its own home, and carried just as gently back to yours.

Mature plants can be imported

Bonsai can be imported from Japan, but they must have all soil removed from the roots, then undergo severe fumigation before they can be allowed to enter this country. It's a great disappointment to buy a tree in Japan and then have it perish from the rigors of agricultural inspection and quarantine. The picture isn't entirely bleak, though, since trees are brought in regularly and many do manage to survive the treatment. (Experienced bonsai cultivators and professional bonsai importers are, of course, the most successful at helping their trees through this very difficult transition. The returning tourist with no prior knowledge of bonsai is more likely to lose his new prize.)

The best time to import trees is during their dormant period, when they are least likely to be harmed by fumigation.

If a plant arrives from out of the country by air (the most expensive way of shipping bonsai), or if it arrives as ship's cargo, arrange for a custom broker to clear it and take it to the agriculture building at the port of entry. Only a broker may handle such a plant until it has been cleared by the proper authorities.

If the tree is brought in on a ship as part of a passenger's baggage, it must first be cleared through customs along with all other baggage. Then one of the ship's personnel must take it to the agriculture building, and the owner may collect it after fumigation.

In both cases, proof of ownership (a customs declaration) is necessary before you can pick up the tree.

When a tree is prepared for such a shipment, all the soil is washed away from its roots, and the roots are then wrapped in damp sphagnum moss. At the port of entry, agricultural inspectors put the tree into a type of gas chamber where it is exposed to methyl bromide, a chemical compound that does away with any diseases and parasites. Unfortunately, diseases and parasites aren't the only victims — the gas also attacks the moisture balance of a tree and tends to dry it out. This is perhaps the greatest danger threatening the survival of imported trees.

After your tree has been properly inspected and fumigated it will be released to you. Get it home promptly and put it outside in a cool place that is well protected from direct sunlight and drafts. Some experts recommend total darkness for the first few days.

To keep your bonsai from further drying out, spray both the foliage and the root ball often with water. Don't attempt to repot the tree immediately — this would require that you unwrap the root ball and expose the roots, causing the tree to dry out even faster. Wait at least 24 hours, keeping the foliage and the root ball damp. This should be enough time to stop the drying out process; then you'll be ready to pot the tree. For specific instructions on potting, turn to page 51.

If you're planning a bonsai-buying trip to Japan, it's a good idea to check with the Plant Quarantine Section of the United States Department of Agriculture before you leave. They'll tell you which trees cannot be imported and which have a poor survival rate on importation. The USDA will also be helpful in giving you further information on customs regulations and on shipping. Of course, checking with bonsai experts, nursery personnel, or importers is worthwhile too.

Planting your bonsai

If your tree isn't in a container, it isn't a bonsai — the Japanese word bonsai literally means "planted in a tray." But it's absolutely essential that both the container and the plant be carefully prepared before planting. Because a tree doesn't normally expect to live in cramped quarters, all conditions must be just right if it's to lead a vigorous and healthy life under these circumstances.

Have everything at hand

ANCHOR SCREEN by bringing wire up through holes, around root ball. Twist wires together to secure.

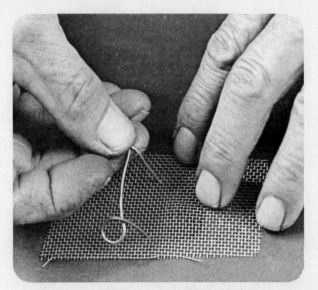

OR secure screen by looping wire as shown, then pushing it through screen and drain hole.

Always do your repotting work away from direct sun and out of any wind, both of which tend to dry out exposed roots. If you plan to repot a nursery plant immediately, have the can cut at the nursery; otherwise, leave it uncut to prevent roots from drying out. Have your tools and materials handy so you don't have to interrupt a delicate operation to go find something. Following are the bare essentials:

• long knife or kitchen spatula, pruning shears, garden trowel

• a couple of chopsticks or other sticks about the size of a pencil, blunt at one end and sharpened at the other

• a bucket half full of water to which you've added a tablespoon of vitamin B_1 mixture

• the new container

• more than enough soil to fill the container when the plant is in it

• sprinkling can or hose nozzle with a spray adjustment

• moss, rocks, lichen, or whatever else you plan to use around the base of the potted tree

Before you do anything with the plant itself, prepare the container. Clean the pot thoroughly. Sterilize pots with chlorine bleach if they have been used before, to kill remnants of any disease that might have been in the soil.

The container must have drain holes in the bottom at least ½ inch in diameter. Cover these with ⅛ to ¼-inch wire mesh so that no soil can escape. If you find a pot you want to use and it has no drain holes, don't despair — here's how to bore a hole in three common materials.

Glass. Build up a small clay well around the area where the hole is to be made. Sprinkle some powdered carborundum in the well and drill the hole with a copper tube clamped in the drill chuck.

Glazed ceramic. Build up a clay well, put a little water in it (to cushion the glaze from the impact of the drill), and use a carbide-tipped bit (available at hardware stores). Or use a copper tube and carborundum, as for glass.

Unglazed pottery. Simply drill the hole, using a carbide-tipped bit. You don't need water here.

Soil is basic

Here's another place where good drainage is vital — the soil you plant your tree in must have it. The roots must be able to get the moisture they need, but if the soil is constantly soggy they will rot. The easiest approach to soil is to use one of the commercial mixes made especially for bonsai. Ask at your nursery about them.

You can also blend a potting mix of your own. A simple mix of sand, peat moss, and earth in equal proportions works well and is easy to prepare.

Use river or quarry sand that you can buy at lumber yards, quarries, or variety stores (under the name of white aquarium sand). Beach sand contains too much salt, even if you wash it thoroughly, and its grain is usually too fine. Sand provides aeration in the mix but no nourishment.

Peat moss is available from any nursery in bags ranging from 1 or 2 cupfuls to several cubic feet. Peat increases the capacity of the soil to hold air and moisture and also keeps the soil from compacting.

Use good garden topsoil for the last ⅓ of the mix. It shouldn't contain large chunks of clay or rock, nor should it have grass roots or weeds in it. Avoid earth from a richly fertilized area such as a vegetable garden; it might be too rich for bonsai.

Whether you're making a potful or a barrelful, mix the ingredients in equal proportions unless you decide to vary the mix as described in the next paragraphs. Dump all the ingredients together and mix well, using a shovel, a garden trowel, or your hands. Be sure to blend in any lumps and pick out twigs and rocks.

Conifers need a slightly drier soil than broadleafed trees. A mix of two parts sand, one part peat, and one part earth allows faster drainage. For broad-leafed trees, mix one part sand, one part peat, and two parts earth to allow for slower drainage.

By matching the soil mixture with the particular needs of the trees, you will create a situation in which you should be able to water all your trees at the same time.

Whether you use a commercial mix or your own mix, start with a layer of gravel or very coarse soil in the bottom of the pot.

As you gain experience with bonsai, you will also gain understanding of the complexities of soil textures. Bonsai experts have done extensive research on soil types, developing very exact data about what combinations of soil textures are best for which plants. You may want to use sieves, as experts do, to screen soil into various grades of coarseness. For the beginner, it's not necessary to be so meticulous, but here is a traditional way of planting bonsai that you can try.

In this method, a coarse soil or gravel forms a layer on the bottom of the container. The pot is then filled about ¾ full with a soil of medium coarseness. Once the tree is in place, more of the medium-coarse soil is added and worked in around the roots. Finally, a very thin layer — a dusting, almost — of fine soil is spread on top. The coarse soil promotes good drainage; the medium soil holds enough water for the roots to use but not enough to get soggy; the fine texture keeps the soil underneath from being disturbed and anchors the roots of the moss on top.

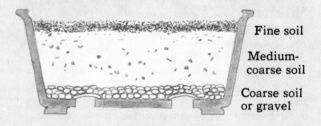

Fine soil

Medium-
coarse soil

Coarse soil
or gravel

Before you transplant

If the can containing a nursery plant isn't cut and you don't have the shears to cut it yourself, slide a long knife blade down and around the inside edge in order to separate the root ball from the sides of the can. Lift the plant out gently by holding the trunk near the base. You may have to work it carefully back and forth a few times. If it doesn't come out, turn the can on its side and strike the edge on a hard surface, being certain to hold the tree's base to prevent it from dropping free.

As soon as you have the plant out of its can, set the root ball in a bucket of water with vitamin B_1 added (follow the label instructions for the exact amount to use). Sprinkle some of the water over the foliage while soaking the root ball.

Slosh the root ball around in the water, working it with your hands to wash soil out from around the roots. Do this until most of the soil is cleared away — if necessary, use a pencil, pointed stick, or chopstick to help remove any hard soil, but be

CHOPSTICK helps clear soil from roots. Check that roots grow from all sides of tree.

CUT ROOT BALL back by ⅓, dipping roots in water as you work to keep them moist.

careful not to break too many of the fine root hairs.

Working the roots in water this way serves several purposes. Both the compacted earth and root ball are softened, and the soil is washed out rather than having to be picked out, which might damage too many delicate roots. The roots stay moist all the time, the vitamin B_1 starts working to stimulate the growth of new root systems, and the liquid helps make the roots flexible — easier to prune and arrange later.

Clear the roots of as much soil as possible without exhausting them and you. It's not necessary to clean away every particle of old soil; a little left in the center of the root mass will do no harm.

Lift the plant out of the water and separate the roots as well as you can. You may have to comb them out with your fingers or with the chopstick. The main thing is to spread out winding and spiraling roots so you can get an idea of their length.

Trimming the roots

For your tree to fit into a shallow container, there must, of course, be no taproot. A taproot is no problem with trees you've propagated yourself, because you will have tended the roots carefully from the very beginning and not allowed a taproot to develop. With gathered trees and some nursery trees, it's another story.

The aim of root trimming is to get rid of much of the older, thicker root material and encourage the growth of new, fine feeder roots, which do the lion's share of the work when it comes to supplying the plant with water and food.

Cut away ⅓ of the total root mass, trimming smoothly around and under. Your cutting should have the effect of flattening the root mass on the bottom and rounding it on the edges. A small taproot

can be cut back by ⅔ or a little more — be sure to make the cut on a slant, not squarely across. If the taproot is large, it will need to be cut back more gradually.

As you do the trimming, dunk the roots occasionally in the water to wash away the loose ones and keep the remaining ones wet. If there are thick, well-developed roots that you plan to expose above the surface, make sure that as you trim you don't cut into or nick any of them. You can cut away extraneous surface roots as long as you don't destroy too many principal ones that support the small feeder roots. The final root mass should cover ⅔ the area of the container. Also, its depth ought to be about ⅓ to ½ the container's height.

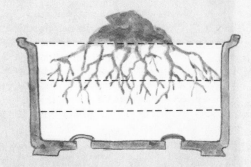

ROOTS should fill about ⅔ container's width and length (above), ⅓ to ½ the depth (below).

Into the pot

The roots are pruned; the soil mix is ready; it's time to plant the tree. But before you put the plant into its container, have clearly in mind how you want it to look. The goal is visual balance, not a symmetrical planting, so use your judgment after studying both tree and container. Here are some guidelines to follow; they aren't absolute rules.

In a rectangular or oval container, place the tree off-center. As the drawing shows, the distance from the base of the tree to the nearest edge of the container should equal about ⅓ the container's length. The tree should stand slightly behind the center line.

LAYER of gravel on bottom of pot helps drainage.

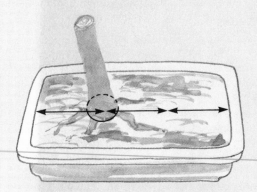

Correct position for a tree placed off-center

If the container you're using is round, square, or hexagonal, center the plant. The exception to this is a cascaded tree, which should be placed slightly off-center. If you're arranging a grove of trees, put the largest tree off-center, again so that the distance from the closest edge of the container is roughly ⅓ the container's length.

Once you know where the tree will go, settle the root mass into the soil, holding the plant steady close to the base. Gently work the roots into the soil a little at a time. As you support the plant with one hand, use the other to add more soil to the pot. A small scoop can help distribute the soil around all the roots. Some experts recommend wiring all trees into their pots as a precaution against up-rooting by wind or by dogs or cats (see page 55).

It's absolutely essential that the area all around the roots be filled in with soil; air pockets are breeding places for rot. The most effective tool for even distribution of soil is a chopstick — use it to work the soil into places where there are air pockets and pack the soil in around the roots. Carry out this operation carefully to avoid damaging the fine root hairs so essential to the plant's health.

FILL POT with soil mix (see page 52 for recipe).

CHOPSTICK helps fill air pockets with soil.

Once the soil is packed firmly and no air pockets remain, establish the level of the soil by adding more or brushing away any excess. The top of this main soil mass should be about ¼ inch below the top of the pot. If you're using three soil textures, here is where you add the layer of fine soil.

To arrange a grove of trees, handle and plant each tree individually. Make sure one is firmly settled into place before planting the next. If the trees are close enough together, you'll probably be able to hold several trees securely with one hand while adding soil with the other (see pages 60-61).

If heavy roots are to be exposed above the surface of the soil, be thorough about pressing and packing soil under and around them after you arrange them. Some roots that belong underground may protrude above the surface. Try pushing them down and covering them with soil. If the weight of the soil doesn't hold them down, you can use a wire clip as shown at right to do the job. Once it's in place, conceal it under the soil. Any tiny root hairs that stick up above the surface can be clipped back.

Some top-heavy trees won't be held down by the soil alone. These need to be held in place by wires, which can be brought up through the bottom of the container as shown at right. Cover these anchoring wires with soil or moss.

As soon as your bonsai is settled in its new pot, submerge the pot in a sink or another large container of water. The water level should come almost to the top of the bonsai pot. Bonsai experts suggest that you use collected rain water or well water on your trees. Bottled distilled water is also good. If you must use tap water, let it stand in the open air for several days to get rid of any chlorine.

The newly potted bonsai should soak for 10 to 15 minutes. While it's soaking, water it from above as well, using a watering can with a fine-spray head. The traditional way to water with a spray head is to simulate rainfall by waving the can up and down as you water (see page 71). This waters the foliage as well as the earth and prevents water from being concentrated in one place.

After potting or repotting, your bonsai is in a condition a bit more delicate than at other times during its normal life. One to 4 weeks of special care will see it through to a more vigorous state.

Keep the newly planted tree protected from extremes of light, heat, wind, and rain. An overhead shelter will keep out direct sun, heavy rain that would wash away soil, and drying wind.

Water the plant moderately the first week or two and spray the foliage often (the hotter the weather, the more you should water both roots and foliage). Don't fertilize your newly potted bonsai for at least a month after its potting; 2 or 3 months is even better.

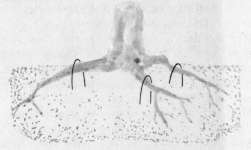

WIRE CLIPS hold down troublesome roots.

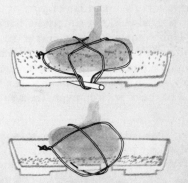

ANCHOR top-heavy tree with wire and stick (above) or use drain holes (below).

Finishing touches

Moss and rocks add natural beauty to your planting. Both take some care and planning to be successfully blended into a newly planted or established bonsai.

Moss

A healthy layer of moss — in addition to helping create a forest effect — keeps the soil in the pot from washing away and helps to conserve soil moisture.

Find moss in damp areas that get little direct sun. In early spring, when the weather is wet, look on the shady sides of garden stones. It's not unusual to find that the edges of brick patios have developed a feathery coating of moss. You'll nearly always find it on large rocks in the woods, along river banks, and on damp retaining walls. Or you can buy dried, powdered moss at a nursery. Use only true moss, not the coarse, long kinds such as Scotch moss that will grow up a tree trunk.

Fit pieces of moss onto the damp soil surface

of the newly planted bonsai, pressing them firmly but gently together where the edges join. Press down the moss around the inside rim of the pot with a small trowel when you're finishing planting. The moss surface should roll or undulate slightly. When the surface is entirely covered, sprinkle the moss with a fine spray of water.

If you use dried moss, sprinkle it over the damp soil, press it into place, and water it down with a fine spray. To keep the moss from washing away, cover it with a sheet of plastic until it has taken root.

Rocks

The same care and judgment that go into every facet of creating a beautiful planting also go into the selection and placement of just the right rock. Before you decide to use a rock with your tree, consider whether or not it really belongs and how it can serve to enhance the feeling and spirit of your planting (see the photos of rock plantings on page 22 and the plant list on page 36).

Most pine and spruce trees and many other evergreens live in the company of fairly rough and rugged rock forms. These rocks have sharp angles, jagged edges, and very often deep clefts. Such rocks appear to be thrusting up out of the earth. If included in a bonsai planting of pine or other evergreens, they should not simply lie flat on the surface or lean complacently against a trunk.

Lower altitude trees such as oaks and maples often grow in the midst of large rocks that have considerably softer, rounder contours than the ones that share a conifer's environment. Trees such as

willows and alders whose habitat is the lowlands or near water are usually at home with very smooth stones.

If you use several rocks in a single planting, try to keep the grain in all of them running in the same direction. They should appear to be part of the same geological formation rather than objects poked here and there with no relation to each other or to the tree.

COLLECTED MOSS must be kept damp with frequent light sprinklings of water.

SPRINKLE powdered moss over damp soil surface. Use fine spray to water.

TAMP powdered moss firmly into soil, in corners, around trees. Plastic cover will help moss take hold.

Special planting techniques

You might want to gain experience with the basic planting just described before you tackle rock, chrysanthemum on a rock, or raft planting.

Chrysanthemum on a rock

One of the beauties of bonsai chrysanthemums is that they come to full maturity in just a year.

Choose a plant with a woody stem and small blossoms — about 1 to 1½ inches in diameter at most — and take cuttings (see pages 39-41). Attach the young chrysanthemum to the rock in February after its first roots have formed. Begin shaping in early spring (once the plant has a strong root system), using basic bonsai training techniques (see pages 62-70) and protecting the plant from frosts.

The cascaded chrysanthemum shown at left was attached to its rock base before shaping began. The drawings below show how the plant was trained onto the rock. Wire and peat muck (see next page) hold the plant in place; plastic wrapped around the rock forms a kind of frame which is filled with potting soil; sphagnum moss is wrapped around the outside of the plastic; and a wire holds everything in place while the roots develop down around the rock. By late April you can start rolling down the bag and removing some of the soil. As the roots grow, continue removing soil until the roots are completely exposed (about mid-July).

When the blossoms fade, cut them back; then move rock and all into a container, surrounding the roots with soil as before. Gradually start cutting back the foliage a few branches at a time until just a few inches of growth remain. Again protecting the plant from frost, begin retraining the branches and gradually exposing the roots when new growth appears.

A chrysanthemum can be retrained like this up to 20 years.

Peter O. Whiteley

1.

2.

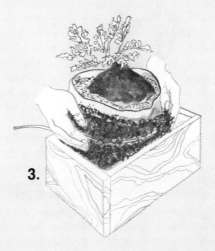

3.

(1) ATTACH WIRE (for training chrysanthemum) and plant to rock with peat muck (see next page); place rock in box and fill with soil. (2) Bottomless plastic bag goes over rock; fill it with soil. (3) Wrap sphagnum moss around plastic; hold in place with wire. Cover moss with newspaper tied with string.

Special plantings

Rock planting

Rocks sometimes actually provide the base of a bonsai planting, in combination with or in place of the soil. The two basic styles are clinging-to-rock, in which the tree grows directly on the rock, and root-over-rock, in which the tree grows over a rock, sending its roots down around the rock and into the soil.

Rough, pitted, craggy rocks are best for clinging-to-rock plantings. The roots must be wired to the rock until they take firm and complete hold, and the rough contours provide excellent anchors for wiring.

Prepare for rock planting by combining half peat moss and half clay with enough water to work it into a pasty texture (called "peat muck"). Also, have large pieces of green moss on hand.

To start, anchor lengths of wire to the rock by drilling a hole as shown on the opposite page, or by using epoxy glue. Then remove almost all the soil from the roots. Holding the plant above the rock, spread all its roots down over the rock very carefully to avoid damaging any of them. Distribute the root material as evenly as you can over the rock — front, back, and sides — to create stability and balance. Or position the roots on the side of the rock as shown.

Cover all the roots with the peat muck and then wire them firmly into place. If the muck does not hold the roots firmly, dip the large pieces of green moss into water and press them into the peak muck. Wrap string or hairpin-shaped copper wires around the green moss to help hold it and the roots. Keep the string on until the moss has taken a firm hold and starts growing — perhaps as long as a year.

For a clinging-to-rock planting, set the rock into a shallow tray with water or damp sand. You'll need to water this kind of planting more often than soil plantings since there is no soil to retain moisture.

A root-over-rock planting is prepared in the same way. Once the tree is fastened to the rock, you prepare your bonsai container with soil just as you do for a regular planting (see page 52). Fill the pot about ¾ full and then gently ease the rock down into it. Bury about ¼ of the rock under the soil and be absolutely certain that all the tree's root ends are beneath the surface, where they will get moisture and food. Finish as you do other plantings with more soil and green moss.

All rock plantings must have extra special care for as much as 2 years because of the drastic root cleaning they undergo. For at least a month — possibly longer, depending on the health of the plant — keep it out of direct sun, wind, and rain, and water it frequently.

Clinging-to-rock planting

FRONT of planting shown on opposite page. Rock, in sand for display, can be kept in saucer of water.

BACK VIEW of same planting. Trees are Shimpaku (or Sargent juniper, Juniperus chinensis sargentii).

1. *SHRUBBY-LOOKING nursery plant has bonsai potential. First, remove it carefully from can.*

2. *WRAP root ball in newspaper to keep it from drying out. Wire and prune as described on pages 62-67.*

3. *SECURE wire in lead split shot or fishing weight; use punch to tap shot into hole drilled in rock.*

4. *REMOVE almost all soil from roots (use wooden chopstick; metal would injure root hairs).*

5. *PRESS thin layer of peat muck on moistened rock where trees will go. Secure trees with wire and muck.*

6. *PEAT MUCK holds moss on rock. Spray water over all. Azalea at right was judged too large, taken out.*

Special plantings

Planting a grove

1. *SEVEN Japanese cryptomeria (Cryptomeria japonica) were pruned and wired (see pages 62-67) in preparation for group planting. Bark was peeled from a few branches of tallest tree to create jin (see page 64). Oval container is good shape for grove planting — though at this point it's hard to believe that all those trees will fit!*

2. *DRAIN HOLES are covered, then first layer of soil goes into pot. Tallest tree is focal point of planting and is placed first — a bit off-center and bit toward front of pot. This tree will sit slightly higher in soil than others.*

3. *PLACEMENT of remaining trees gets special attention. Second tree is slightly in front to make first tree look bigger. Smaller trees at back add depth. Expert is checking to see if root ball needs additional cutting to fit.*

60

4. *WIGGLE wooden chopstick between roots to settle soil in air holes. Use tools or rocks to hold trees in place before soil goes in. Soil level should be uneven so not all trees are at same height; spacing between trees should be unequal, too. Final touches are moss (powdered moss was sprinkled over soil) and judicious pruning. (If branches merge, prune the back branches of the more forward tree.)*

5. *MINIATURE FOREST emerges from planting. Upright trees are best for this style; choose those that naturally grow in groves or forests: maple, beech, birch, spruce, and zelkova. All the same kind is most effective. Because pattern of trees is more important in group planting than any one tree, choose plants that will complement each other and save more unusual specimens for single plantings.*

Raft planting

A fine grove of trees is surprisingly easy — you can create one from a single specimen by planting one tree on its side and letting its branches become the grove. Japanese maples and the Japanese white pines lend themselves well to this "raft" style of planting (see the photo of a raft planting at the top of page 21).

Start with a tree that has a well-developed trunk and several good-size branches growing somewhat straight out from the trunk. Keeping several main branches along one side, cut off all other branches on the tree, leaving small stumps. Thin the roots.

Now plant the tree on its side, with the cut stumps down and the remaining branches up, leaving a little of the trunk exposed above the surface. Flatten the thinned-out root ball into the soil and cover it by heaping more soil over it. (You may have to wire it down to keep it low.) Don't cover the trunk completely, but press moss up to it in a natural manner. In time each of the former branches will develop into a main trunk to form a grove of trees.

Special plantings

As the twig is bent

A true bonsai, of course, is more than just an artificially dwarfed plant, more than just a tree in a tray. It is a plant that has been not only dwarfed, but carefully trained and shaped — this is where the bonsai enthusiast uses his knowledge of plants to establish and control the form they will take. It isn't enough just to know when and where to prune any more than it is enough just to have "good taste." You need both, and both will come to you as you work with, study, and enjoy your bonsai.

Pruning and wiring — and sometimes tying, propping, and using jacks and weights — are techniques for training your plants discussed in the following section.

When should training begin?

Start training a bonsai only when you're certain the plant is vigorous enough to tolerate various rigors without dying. Experts suggest that graftings, seedlings, and cuttings are strong enough when they've produced new shoots 2 to 3 inches long. Layerings ought to have plenty of new shoots and leaves. Gathered trees will already have waited 2 years before being placed in bonsai pots, and they can begin training as soon as they have had a chance to establish themselves soundly in their new homes.

A strong nursery tree may be ready for training after only a month or two in its bonsai pot. If the foliage shows no signs of drooping or discoloring at that point, consider your bonsai hardy enough to begin training.

How to prune bonsai

You'll do two kinds of pruning on your bonsai — one is drastic pruning, the other is nipping or pinching back. The chart on pages 76-77 gives information about when to prune and pinch some of the more common bonsai plants.

Pruning is normally just a one-time operation, performed on gathered trees or nursery trees (and occasionally on established bonsai when damage or disease creates a need for altering the basic shape). Pruning establishes the basic shape of a plant by removing nonessential and unsightly branches. Before you start, study the tree carefully to decide which branches to remove.

Two things need to be considered when you're doing drastic pruning — the health of the tree and the possibility of leaving scars. Never prune if there's any question at all about the vitality of the plant. Drastic pruning can be enough to kill an unhealthy tree.

The seasonal care chart (pages 76-77) gives more information about when to prune some specific bonsai plants.

1. To prevent or at least minimize scarring as a result of drastic pruning, always try to leave the pruned wood with a concave surface. Use a trimmer (see page 75) to cut off the branch as close to flush as possible. Next, get a small chisel and cut off more wood until the surface is concave (A) or at least flush (B). New bark will grow, rolling over the cut area and most often blending in evenly with the old bark. Leaving the cut lumpy or stubby would make the area vulnerable to rotting or create an unsightly patch of dead wood (C).

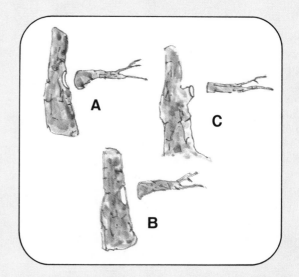

2. When you trim a large branch, leave a "heel" of bark from the under portion of the branch as shown. The length of the heel should be equal to the diameter of the branch being removed. Cut the branch off flush or a little concave; then cover the cut with the heel and tie it in place with raffia until the cut mends (probably a few weeks).

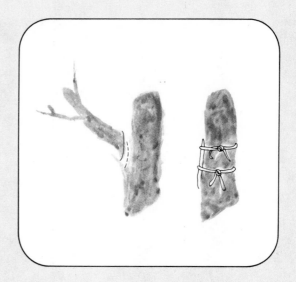

Pinching back is a means of controlling new growth before it becomes woody and demands drastic pruning; best of all, it won't leave any scars. Unlike drastic pruning, which is normally a one-time-only operation, pinching back is a continuing necessity. It's this technique that gives you fine control over the plant's size and shape. Pinching back makes a gawky, twiggy tree more dense. Nipping all the terminal buds on a branch will force several side branches to grow. Done all over, nipping creates a bushy plant.

Proper pinching back also controls the direction of growth (see below). Leave on all buds that point in the direction you want new growth; remove all others. Usually you will pinch back all inward growing buds and leave selected outside ones that enhance the shape of the tree. The bottoms or branches should be clean with no downward-growing shoots.

You can do the pinching back with your fingers or with tweezers. Be especially careful to touch no other new growth except what you're removing. New growth is injured very easily and dies quickly.

In general, trees may be pinched back any time during the growing season as new growth appears. Most pines grow slowly enough that you'll pinch them back only once a season. Other conifers such as Sargent juniper and cypress need to be pinched back constantly during the growing season. Pinch back flowering trees and fruit trees right after they have bloomed, well before the middle of the growing season.

Tiny spurs that appear on the trunk or along heavy branches can be rubbed off with your fingers. If left on, they may develop into long, unsightly suckers that will leave a scar when removed later.

TAKE CARE in pinching — don't harm other growth.

CONTROL GROWTH by pinching back all buds except those that point upward.

Pruning

CREATE JIN by scraping off foliage, using dull knive that will not cut into wood. Here, apex is scraped. Then a lower branch is wired to become new apex.

Age can be simulated

Rather than pruning a branch tip or the top of a tree, you can create *jin*, a portion of dead wood that gives a tree the appearance of great age (see page 23).

Carefully peel the bark off the appropriate branch. The wood you expose will die and eventually turn gray like dead wood on very old forest trees. You can hasten the wood's discoloration by wiping it with a little lime sulphur, but be very careful not to get any on the living portions of the plant.

Leaf cutting

Leaf cutting is a technique used to enhance the appearance of broadleaf evergreens and most deciduous trees — except flowering or fruiting trees. Its purpose is to accelerate growth and to reduce the size of a plant's leaves.

Leaf cutting is actually defoliation of a plant. By removing all of a tree's leaves you create a false autumn. Soon after, new growth begins to appear. What you've done is squeeze two growing seasons into one. On young trees, leaf cutting accelerates growth but doesn't significantly reduce leaf size. On older trees, leaf size may be substantially reduced by leaf cutting.

The correct time for leaf cutting is early summer through midsummer. Do it too early in spring (before the end of May or the beginning of June) and the second-growth leaves will be larger than the first ones, not smaller; do it too late (after mid-August) and the tree may fail to resprout. (Leaf cutting can also be done when off-season transplanting is necessary. By stripping the tree of all its leaves, you reduce transplant shock.)

Avoid fertilizing the tree right before or after leaf cutting. Cut the leaves as shown below, removing the entire leaf but leaving the stem. If any portion of the leaf is left on, the tree will spend its energy on it instead of on building new leaves.

The new leaves should begin to appear about a month after the old ones have been removed. Until new buds appear, keep the tree in a shady place. Without leaves to transpire moisture, the tree will need much less watering than normal.

LEAF CUTTING requires removal of entire leaf. Only stem should remain.

The fine control of form

The pruning and pinching operations described for bonsai are nothing new to garden plant enthusiasts — the techniques are the same for most kinds of plants. But the wiring and bending of branches to give form and shape to a plant is unique to bonsai.

Wiring to shape a tree

Wiring can make a young tree look old by turning branches downward. It can turn an upright tree into a cascade, add a curve to a straight trunk, or create a new apex out of a strong branch.

Wiring must be done with care since it usually takes place after a tree has been thinned, and the branches that remain are crucial to the design of the tree. The best way to learn to wire is to try it several times with a large, fairly limber branch pruned from a garden tree.

When to wire specific plants is detailed in the seasonal care chart on pages 76-77. In general, deciduous trees are wired in the growing season after leaves are full size but while branches are still easily bent. Wire evergreens in fall or winter. Some other plants, such as azaleas, are less brittle when dormant and might be wired better in winter. Never wire plants in the budding season; it's too easy to damage the young buds.

Two kinds of wire work well for bonsai. Traditionally, bonsai experts have used copper wire. But aluminum wire with a dull finish is available too and perfectly suitable for bonsai wiring. It's flexible, easy to bend, holds bends well, and doesn't rust.

Look for wire at nurseries and hardware stores. The size you use will depend on the thickness of the branch or trunk to be wired. Number 8 wire is heavy and should be used only for a trunk since it would put too much weight on a branch. Number 16 and smaller are light and should be used for very thin branches or for tying rather than bending.

For bonsai work, copper wire is often annealed to make it more flexible. The Japanese masters anneal by putting the bare wire in a hot fire kindled with rice straw. If you want to anneal your own wire, make a fire of tightly wrapped newspapers and put the wire in it. After the flames have cooled from redhot to blue, remove the wire and let it cool. Don't bend it before you're ready to use it.

As a general rule, the wire you use should be about ⅓ the thickness of the branch at its thickest point. The length of a given piece of wire should be about half again as long as the branch to be wired.

Once a branch has taken on its trained form you can remove the wire and reuse it. Straighten out the twists and bends and flatten it by tapping it with a mallet.

Before you begin wiring, it's a good idea to let a plant go without water for a day, making the branches more limber and easier to bend. This is especially important with deciduous trees, whose branches tend to break more easily when bent. Have the proper gauges and lengths of wire on hand, and know what parts of the tree you will bend and how you want to bend them.

Just before you start to wrap the wire around the trunk or branches, bend them carefully, a little bit at a time, until they take the shape you want them to have. If it seems they won't bend in the way you want them to without breaking, you can make a small cut in them as shown below to help in bending. Never wire shoots that are less than 2 inches long; they're tender and too easy to damage. Protect soft-barked trees such as maple and beech by wrapping the wires with paper.

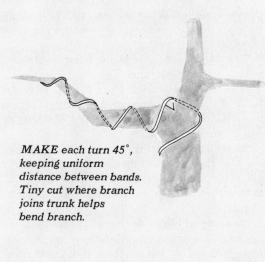

MAKE each turn 45°, keeping uniform distance between bands. Tiny cut where branch joins trunk helps bend branch.

PROTECT very tender bark by wrapping wire with paper.

Wiring technique

To wire the trunk, anchor the end of the wire in the soil, pushing it down to the bottom of the pot. Do this at the back of the trunk, so the wire won't show. Wire diagonally clockwise or counterclockwise, and wrap the wire in 45° turns, keeping a uniform distance between bands. Keep the winding snug but not too tight. If the wire is too loose, the trunk or branch won't hold a bend; if it's too tight, the bark may be damaged. Remember that the wire will tighten as you bend the trunk or branch.

When you move from wiring the trunk to wiring branches you may continue without cutting the wire if the branches are large, or finish off and start again with smaller wire. The end of a wire should blend in with the trunk or branch — hidden in back if possible. Cut it off and press the end close against the bark so it doesn't stick out.

<u>Where to start.</u> Always begin at the lowest point to be wired, whether it's on the trunk or a main branch, and work up from the heaviest branches to the lightest branches. Begin at the junction of the branch and trunk or at a major branch fork and secure the wire by wrapping it around the trunk or branch. Always face the end of the branch you are wiring. When wiring branches, take special care not to bend or break leaves, small shoots, or branches.

The photos on the opposite page illustrate the proper wiring technique. The right hand guides the wire around the branch while the left hand follows, holding the coils tight against the wood. You may use a double strand of wire for added strength, but never crisscross wires.

As you do the wiring, it's a good idea to begin bending the branch in the direction you want it to go, in preparation for the final bend. Once a branch is wired properly you can bend it into its new shape.

Before you begin, decide what form you want the branch to take. Once you have put a bend in a branch, don't try to straighten it or bend it in a different direction. Doing so would weaken the wood greatly and make it more likely to split.

Keep both thumbs together on the inside of the bend and hold the branch firmly. It is best not to have a section of wire right inside a bend since it has very little holding power there. Make the bends quite gradual, and don't attempt any sharp angles or corners.

<u>Unlucky breaks.</u> On occasion, no matter how meticulously you have wired a branch or how gently you have formed it, it will snap. Azalea, sweet gum (*liquidambar*), and persimmon are notorious for this. If the branch doesn't come completely apart, there's a chance you can save it.

(Continued on page 68)

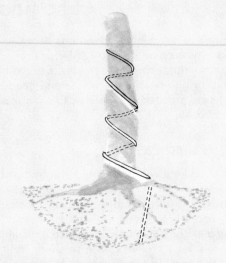

START WIRING at lowest point on tree and work upward and outward. Here, wire is anchored in soil.

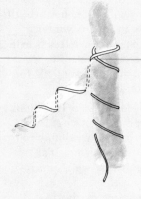

REAR of tree shows wire secured by crossing.

FROM FRONT of tree, crossed wire should not be visible.

How to wire bonsai

1.   **2.**   **3.**

(1) TREE BEFORE WIRING has almost straight trunk, upward-growing branches, not much character. (2) To anchor wire, push it all the way down into root ball. (3) Wrap wire up trunk, spacing turns evenly. Number 14 wire is right size for this trunk.

4.   **5.**   **6.**

(4) TO BEND TRUNK, gently push with thumb while pulling toward you with other hand. (5) Face branch to be wired, start at trunk, and wrap wire out to tip. Use thinner wire on smaller branches, wiring smallest branches very carefully. (6) Greatest downward curve is on older, bottom branches; new growth at top of tree doesn't taper.

Training

Fixing a broken branch

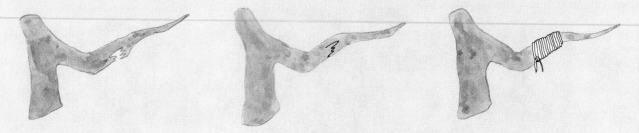

EASE BROKEN BRANCH back together; wrap branch with raffia or garden tape.

...Continued from page 66

Very gently ease it back at the breaking point until the broken pieces of the branch fit together exactly. Wrap the break with raffia or with garden tape and tie it up. The fracture should heal in about 2 months. If a branch snaps off entirely, though, there is nothing you can do except prune back the stub (see page 62 for pruning instructions).

In shaping wired branches, avoid crossing or intermingling them. You might be able to twist a branch to one side to help fill in a gap, but don't distort it into an unnatural shape. A ragged, sparse tree will often be helped by having its branches bent into open spaces. But if during pruning too much wood has been removed, wiring and bending will be of little help.

After you wire a tree, keep it out of direct sunlight for 2 to 4 days and give it plenty of water. The foliage should have a daily sprinkling during this period. Because small, invisible cracks may develop during the bending process, it's a good idea to keep the plant out of direct wind for at least 2 weeks until any cracks have had time to heal.

You can leave the wire on young deciduous trees for about 3 or 4 months. Older deciduous trees grow much more slowly than young ones, and pines also grow quite slowly; leave the wire on these for at least a year. If the wire is left on too long, though, the tree's bark will begin to grow around it. This not only makes it difficult to remove the wire, but also leaves large, unsightly scars on the plant.

To remove a wire, start at the outermost end of a branch and unwind back toward the anchor end. Be careful not to harm leaves or small shoots and branches. If the wire has been on so long that it has begun to cut into the bark, don't try to unwind it — you might accidentally tear off some of the bark. Use a small wire cutter to snip the wire off in small pieces.

Other training techniques

Wiring has no monopoly where bonsai training is concerned; other methods are also effective in establishing the form of a tree. A branch that's too stiff for bending by wiring can often be bent by tying. Branches can be tied with thinner wire than that used for wiring and bending. Never knot or twist a wire tightly onto a branch, but make a very loose loop and protect the wood by slipping a small pad under the wire.

In tying or propping, don't try to force a branch into its new position all at once — especially if the change from its original form is a radical one. It may split or break. Secure it at ⅓ to ½ the full final position, wait 2 or 3 months, and then pull it a little more. Continue to do this until you achieve the desired form.

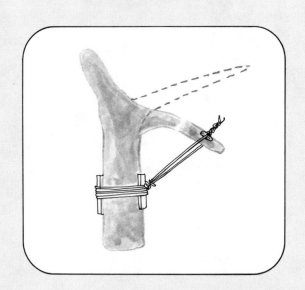

Several branches can be pulled downward to give a weeping appearance. You do this by running lengths of tie wire from each branch to the base of the tree. Secure the wires to the trunk, to the pot, or to exposed thick roots if possible.

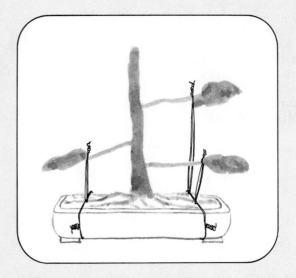

A variation of tying branches involves using a weighted string or wire to hold the branch down. As the illustration shows, you simply attach a weight to a string or wire and affix the other end to the branch you want drawn downward. Choose the weight carefully; if it's too heavy it will snap the branch. There are weights made specifically for this purpose. You can also use stones or lead fish-line weights.

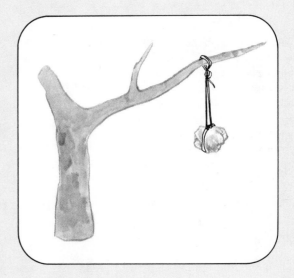

Maybe your tree has a pair of forked branches or two trunks or branches that are too close together and you can find no way of attaching wires to pull them apart. In that case, you can prop them apart with a small twig or dowel. Cut a small notch in each end of the prop and wedge the stick between the two branches to force them apart. Remove the prop after 3 or 4 months. If the branches spring back to their original positions, put the prop back. Eventually they will lose their tendency to spring back when the prop is removed.

(Continued on next page)

Training

. . . Continued from page 69

To train a pair of branches or trunks closer together, bend a small piece of wire into an "S" shape. Hook each branch onto one of the curves of the "S" to draw the two together. Eventually you can remove the "S" and the branches will stay in their new position.

Changing the shape of a heavy trunk usually requires more than just wiring. Special bonsai jacks can help do this, but it is tricky and a beginner would benefit from a bonsai expert's first-hand guidance.

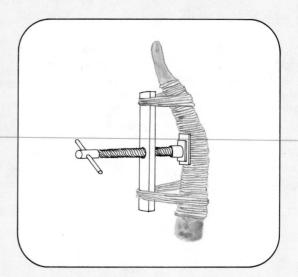

A certain amount of care

It is a common misconception that bonsai are tortured and neglected. This is far from true. Once it has been potted properly, a bonsai thrives on a fairly simple regime of careful watering, occasional feeding, a little winter protection, and a watchful eye for pests.

Your first consideration is where to keep your bonsai. Though very small, a bonsai is still a forest-type tree, an outdoor tree, and only outdoors will it be subject to the cycle of the seasons as it would be in its natural state. It can be brought inside under certain circumstances (see page 78), but normally it should be kept outside, above the ground on a shelf or bench to protect it from dogs and cats.

As an outdoor plant it likes what all outdoor plants like — sunlight, fresh air, and water. Very important to a bonsai's health is the avoidance of any extremes. Heavy winds may damage, even break, branches; intense heat and sunlight may burn foliage; heavy and continuous rains can wash away soil and perhaps cause roots to rot.

Keep the plant where it can get plenty of sunlight, but protect it from strong afternoon sun in summer. Avoid putting it near a wall that will reflect a lot of heat, and turn it occasionally so all sides get good sunlight. Be certain it gets generous air circulation — gentle breezes won't hurt. A spot under the eaves or a garden tree is ideal; so is a place sheltered by lathwork or by bamboo or synthetic screening. It should be protected from downpours.

Watering--let your plant guide you

The watering of bonsai is really quite simple. Often an inexperienced gardener's anxieties about the survival of his plant get translated into over-watering — and too much watering can be as harmful to the health of the tree as too little water-ing. At the very least, overwatering causes excess growth which is likely to ruin the carefully con-trolled shape of the tree. At worst it encourages root rot which will eventually kill the tree.

Since a bonsai exists in a very small container, its soil holds little water in reserve and therefore it must be watered regularly. The rule is simple — water the plant when the soil is dry. Poke your finger into the earth below the surface moss. When the moisture is gone, it's time to water. Soon you'll develop a watering routine, and your bonsai will readily adapt to it. When the weather is extremely hot you may need to water twice a day — once in the early morning and once in the evening. Mild weather may mean watering just three or four times a week. Until you're certain you know the plant's needs, keep checking the soil and let that guide you.

Chlorine and other additives in tap water can harm a bonsai, so it's best to use well water, rain water (set out a large container to collect it), or distilled water. If you must use tap water, fill a container with it and let it stand outside for a few days first. Another benefit of this is that the sun will bring the water to the same temperature as the plant; cold water can be a shock to bonsai.

The traditional way to water bonsai is to use the kind of watering can pictured below. It has a fine-spray head at the end of its spout. Wave the can up and down over the plant so the fine spray of water falls onto the tree, through the foliage, and onto the soil just as rain would. This technique cleans and cools the foliage.

You can also water the soil directly with a water-ing can. When you do this, be certain to water all around the plant, not just in front. Water until the soil is saturated — that is, until water begins running out of the drainage hole at the bottom.

If your collection grows to include a large number of plants, you might want to use the water-ing device pictured on the next page. Controlled from a single spigot, it can water any number of plants at once.

Another way to water bonsai is from the bottom up. Set bonsai pots in a large container of water, the level just below the top of the bonsai pots. Let them stand in the water about 15 minutes while moisture soaks upward through the soil. When dampness reaches the top of the soil, it is saturated thoroughly. Constant use of this method may cause salts to accumulate on the container, so use it only occasionally for a thorough soaking.

If you water the soil directly, you'll also need to mist the foliage regularly to help keep the plant clean and cool. In moderate weather mist the foliage three or four times a week. When the days are hot, spray at least once a day, or more if the

TRADITIONAL bonsai watering can has spray as fine as light rain.

Care

DRIP irrigation system uses plastic tubing attachments to keep bonsai constantly moist. Collar (above) is harder to dislodge and distributes water more evenly around plant than spaghetti tubes (right), but it has no individual turnoff device. Both are part of commercially available system.

foliage looks parched and droopy. Mist in the morning or in late afternoon, but not when the sun is at its hottest, for drops of water left on the leaves will cause leaves to burn.

Misting the foliage helps control temperature and keeps leaves clean and healthy. In large metropolitan areas, smog may affect some plants — broad-leafed plants in particular. Maples in smoggy areas, for instance, may leaf out beautifully in the spring, only to have their leaves start turning brown at the edges, then shrivel altogether. Keeping the leaves sprayed clean may not prevent all smog damage, but it's just about the only thing you can do.

Some general rules on watering your bonsai follow. More important than rules, though, is your awareness of the special habits and needs of your plants; let them be your guides.

Spring. In early spring, water once a day in the morning. It's particularly important not to water at night if you live in an area that might still be getting frost. In late spring you may find some of your plants using so much water that they'll need watering twice a day — in morning and again in late afternoon.

Summer. In extremely hot weather, some trees may need to be watered as much as three times a day. Water once in the morning, once at midday, and once in late afternoon. Normally, though, twice daily is enough, as outlined in the preceding paragraph.

Fall. One watering a day, or once every other day, is usually suitable in fall's cooler weather as your plants' growing slows with the approach of winter.

Winter. Because life forces in the plants are minimal in winter, a watering every other day should suffice. Check the soil for moisture before you water. (For more information on winter care, see page 73.)

The most trying time for you and your bonsai is when you leave home for more than a few days. The bonsai enthusiast may find it's as difficult to leave his trees in the care of another as it is to leave his children or his pets. If you'll be gone for only 3 to 5 days, encase your bonsai pot in a clear plastic bag and keep it in the shade. It should keep well until you return.

For longer vacations, prepare a list of very specific watering instructions for each plant so that the person caring for them will have no doubts about what to do. Obviously it's best to ask another bonsai hobbyist to care for your plants, but that isn't always possible. Some people take their trees to a local nursery for care, like taking a poodle to a kennel.

Nourishment is necessary

Like all other living things, a bonsai needs nourishment to stay alive. Proper fertilizing keeps the plant healthy, promotes lush growth, and helps the plant resist disease. Bonsai experts recommend natural organic fertilizers rather than chemical ones: blood meal, fish meal, cotton seed, rape seed, bone meal, or aged animal manure are all good, though animal manure needs to be diluted to prevent burning the roots.

Many bonsai hobbyists make their own fertilizer mixes, combining such ingredients as cottonseed oil, fish oil, wood ash, chicken manure, bone meal, and blood meal in correct proportions to satisfy the particular needs of their plants. (Nitrogen is especially important for leaf growth; fruits and flowers like more potassium and phosphorous.)

For most bonsai you can use a liquid fertilizer like fish emulsion or an organic house plant food. Follow precisely the label instructions for diluting; don't be tempted to make the solution any richer. As mild as house plant fertilizers are, they can harm the delicate roots of a bonsai if used in too concentrated a form. It's always better to overdilute than underdilute. Use a small watering can to apply liquid fertilizer, saturating the soil. Keep applying until water runs out the drainage hole in the bottom of the pot. Don't get any fertilizer on the foliage; it may burn.

In general, fertilize your bonsai once a month. Avoid fertilizing them at all, though, for a month or two during hot weather. In the fall and winter use a fertilizer with a nitrogen-phosphorus-potassium ratio such as 0-10-10 or 2-10-10; in the spring use a fertilizer with a higher proportion of nitrogen. If a bonsai's leaves begin to yellow or spot, it means some trace minerals are missing. This shouldn't happen if you're using an all-purpose fertilizer containing copper, iron, zinc, and other trace minerals. If yellowing occurs, substitute an all-purpose product for whatever other fertilizer you might be using.

Winter care

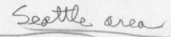
Seattle area

If you're fortunate enough to live in an area that has mild winters, frequent rains, and occasional sunlight, your bonsai will be cared for by the elements themselves and will actually need less attention in winter than during the rest of the year. If your trees have some kind of shelter overhead — even the foliage of a garden tree — frosts will seldom bother them. About all you have to do is keep the soil well watered.

Where winters are severe, bonsai care is another story. Here bonsai trees do need more attention, but still they needn't be overly pampered. Even in the hardest winters, don't keep bonsai in a greenhouse. Doing so may force unseasonal growth, and like all trees, bonsai need a dormant period. Good air circulation is more important than warmth.

If you have some sort of lath house arrangement for your trees, put up side shelters during the winter that will give protection from frost but still allow fresh air movement. In Japan, wooden frames with straw matting are used. Inexpensive roll-up bamboo blinds will work if you brace them against strong winds.

You can build a simple coldframe by digging a hole about 1½ feet deep in the earth, making it as long and as wide as you need for all of your plants. (Do this before the ground is frozen.) Line the sides but not the bottom with exterior grade plywood, which should extend 6 inches above the surface. Put 4 to 6 inches of gravel in the bottom of the hole, set your containers on the gravel, and then spread straw around and over them. Add a loose-fitting top made from old window panes or polyethylene sheeting that will let in light. (For other coldframe ideas and plans see the *Sunset* books *Basic Gardening Illustrated* and *Garden Work Centers*.) Coldframe kits are available that are both inexpensive and easy to assemble. Check with local nurseries or see the catalogues of mail-order garden supply houses.

During cold winter months, water your trees in the morning so the water will drain out during the day. If water stands in the soil at night and freezes, it could destroy roots or crack the container.

COLDFRAME made from old window protects bonsai during coldest winters.

Root pruning established bonsai

Root pruning serves two purposes — it keeps the root system within the bounds of the container and it encourages the growth of fine feeder roots. Both results improve drainage and aeration. Both are conducive to the plant's receiving better nourishment. The finer the roots, the more of them can be contained in the pot without crowding. The more uncrowded root surface, the better the plant is fed.

It's easy to check a tree for a potbound condition. Around January or February, let the plant go without water for a day, so the soil will dry out. Hold the container firmly with one hand, and, grasping the trunk with the other, lift it gently out of the pot. Be sure you don't jerk it out. Look at the root system. If it's packed tightly in the form of the inside of the pot and there seems to be no space at all in the root mass for soil, then the plant is probably crowded and should be repotted. If there seems to be a fair amount of breathing space between roots, or if you can see only a few roots in the soil, then all is well.

This apparently rough treatment does no harm to the plant. Of course, you can't do this with a tree that is growing in a rock or one that has several rocks around its base. With these, inspect the edges of the soil or the drain holes in the bottom of the container every year or so. If you see a *lot* of roots poking out (not just one or two), it's a fair sign that things are getting a little crowded.

To readapt an established bonsai to its container, remove any surface rocks and then take off the moss in pieces as large as possible. Mist the moss and wrap it in a plastic bag. By keeping it damp, you'll be able to use it again after you've finished repotting the tree. Tilt or invert the container and shake it firmly to loosen the root ball. Removing it will be much easier if you let it go without water the day before.

An established bonsai plant should keep some of its original soil. Begin by cutting away ⅓ of the plant's root ball — soil and roots — using a knife or shears. When you cut roots, always cut them at about a 45° downward slant; this allows them to heal much faster.

After you've removed ⅓ of the plant's root ball, take a pencil or a chopstick and remove half the remaining soil from around the roots. As you do this, be really careful to avoid damaging remaining roots.

Next, remove all downward growing roots. Try to flatten the root ball on the bottom and cut so that its final thickness is about ⅓ the height of the container.

Finally, thin the remaining soil by removing sections as if you were removing every other piece of a pie.

Keep a watchful eye

In addition to monitoring the general health of your trees, you should watch for the growth of weeds in the container. Weeds detract from the appearance of a plant and rob the soil of nourishment that should go to the tree. Use the tool shown below for pulling weeds. If a weed is so large that uprooting it might disturb the soil, hold down the soil around it and then pull it up.

Keep the surface of the soil clean by brushing away dead leaves or needles; you can also use tweezers for this. Be careful not to tear up any moss.

Dead leaves on the surface of a bonsai container can harbor insects — another good reason for not letting leaves accumulate. The most common bonsai pests are aphids, red spider mites, scale insects, snails, slugs, sowbugs, pillbugs, and earwigs. You can deal with most insects quickly and effectively — just spray them off with a jet of water. If the infestation persists, spray the foliage with a strong solution of pyrethrum and nicotine, available from your local nursery. Never use this solution in the budding season.

If ants or other insects have made nests in the soil, repot the bonsai right away, removing all the old soil and soaking the roots in a weak pyrethrum solution for a few minutes.

You'll need these tools

For bonsai work, the basic tools are few and relatively inexpensive. You may already have some of them around the house or garden. If not, you can easily find them at most nurseries or garden supply stores.

In addition to the tools shown at the right, tweezers (shown on the opposite page) are handy for nipping buds and removing weeds, dropped needles, and leaves from the surface of the soil. The best watering can to use is the kind pictured on page 71 — one with a long nozzle and fine-spray head for watering in the traditional way. If you water the soil by soaking, you'll also need a sprayer for misting the foliage.

Hook-and-blade pruning shears are preferable to the anvil type; they make a clean, close cut, whereas anvil shears leave a little stub and sometimes crush the cut end in the process. Wire cutters and a garden trowel for filling containers will also be useful.

Pictured at right are these tools:
A. Trimmer for twigs and buds
B. Trimming shears for branches and roots
C. Brush for cleaning and smoothing topsoil
D. Nipper that leaves a concave depression when cutting a branch
E. Smaller trimming shears for buds, twigs, leaves, and exposed roots

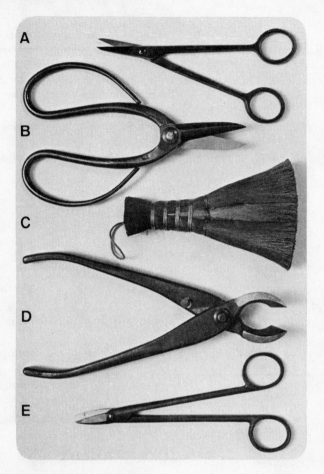

Bonsai work centers

Bonsai makes only modest demands on work space, but you should at least have a spot where you can spill dirt and drop cuttings without worrying about the mess. A corner of a porch or patio — even a small outside balcony — will work well. You should have good light, but don't work in direct sun. When a plant is out of a container and you're working on the roots, they can dry out fast. During warm summer months, a temporary bench set up under a shady tree is ideal, and you won't have to worry about spilling dirt.

The drawings on page 79 show some basic work center possibilities. (See also the *Sunset* book *Garden Work Centers.*) Any of these can be adapted to bonsai use.

If you plan a permanent work center, you will want a wooden bench at least 3 feet high (for sitting; higher for standing), 6 feet long, and 3 feet wide. This is enough surface to allow you to scatter tools, containers, and plant material while working.

You can supplement it with shelves for a display, or you can display your trees in a separate area (see page 78 for a discussion of displaying trees). Under the main workbench you can have bins for soil and more shelves for storing containers, pots, and rocks. A box or small galvanized can for trash comes in handy. Try to have a water supply available to save yourself steps in filling and refilling a container.

A useful device in a bonsai work center is a turntable (see photo page 32) that lets you view all sides of a plant easily without having to walk around it or continually lift and turn it. Tools can be kept handy in one place if there's a drawer under the turntable.

Once you become engrossed in working with a plant, you'll be bending, twisting, and craning to see it from every possible angle. Keep a small stool handy, one that will bring your head to the height of the plant when you sit down.

Care

Seasonal care chart

Genus	Pinching	Pruning	Wiring and Bending	Potting and Root Pruning
Abies Fir	Spring	Spring-Summer	Any time	Spring[4]
Acer Maple	Spring-Summer	Spring	Spring-Autumn[3]	Winter-Spring
Bamboo Bamboo	Spring-Summer	Spring-Summer	Don't wire	Spring-Summer
Camellia Camellia	Summer-Winter[1]	Summer-Winter	Summer-Winter	Spring-Summer
Cedrus Cedar	Spring & Autumn	Any time	Any time	Spring[4]
Celtis Hackberry	Spring-Summer	Spring-Summer	Spring-Autumn[3]	Winter-Spring
Chaenomeles Flowering quince	Spring-Summer	Spring-Summer	Any time	Spring
Chamaecyparis False cypress	Spring & Autumn	Any time	Any time	Any time[4]
Cornus Dogwood	Summer-Winter[1]	Summer	Spring-Autumn[3]	Spring
Cotoneaster Cotoneaster	Spring-Summer	Spring-Summer	Spring-Summer	Spring-Summer
Crataegus Hawthorn	Summer[1]	Summer	Spring-Autumn[3]	Spring
Cryptomeria Cryptomeria	Spring & Autumn	Spring-Summer	Spring-Summer	Spring[4]
Cupressus Cypress	Spring & Autumn	Any time	Any time	Spring[4]
Diospyros Persimmon	Summer-Autumn[1]	Summer	Spring-Autumn[3]	Spring-Summer
Fagus Beech	Spring-Summer	Spring-Summer	Spring-Autumn[3]	Spring
Fraxinus Ash	Summer-Autumn	Summer-Autumn	Spring-Autumn[3]	Spring
Ginkgo Maidenhair tree	Spring-Summer	Spring-Summer	Any time	Spring
Hedera Ivy	Spring-Summer	Spring-Summer	Any time	Spring
Ilex Holly	Spring-Summer	Spring-Summer	Spring-Summer	Spring

This chart shows the best times of year to train and repot your bonsai. If you don't see a particular plant listed here, follow the guidelines for the same type of tree; for example, a broad-leafed deciduous tree would be treated much like a maple; a conifer, like a pine.

Details about all these operations are on pages 62-74. Fertilizing should be done monthly except in the hottest weather.

The four seasons are defined as follows:
Spring: March, April, May
Summer: June, July, August
Autumn: September, October, November
Winter: December, January, February
When a range of seasons is given such as Winter-Spring, it means that the operation can be done in late winter (February) or early spring (March).

Genus	Pinching	Pruning	Wiring and Bending	Potting and Root Pruning
Jasminum Jasmine	Spring & Autumn	Summer-Autumn	Spring-Summer	Spring-Autumn
Juniperus Juniper	Spring & Autumn	Any time	Any time	Spring[4]
Larix Larch	Spring & Autumn	Any time	Any time[3]	Winter-Spring
Malus Crabapple	Summer	Summer	Spring-Summer[3]	Spring-Autumn[5]
Picea Spruce	Spring	Spring-Summer	Autumn-Winter	Spring[4]
Pinus Pine	Spring	Summer	Autumn-Winter	Spring[4]
Prunus Flowering fruits	Summer-Autumn[1]	Winter-Spring[2]	Spring-Summer[3]	Winter-Spring[6]
Punica Pomegranate	Spring & Autumn	Spring-Summer	Spring-Summer	Spring-Summer
Pyracantha Firethorn	Spring & Autumn	Spring-Summer	Any time	Spring
Quercus Oak	Spring & Autumn	Summer-Winter	Spring-Autumn[3]	Spring
Rhododendron Azalea	Summer	Summer	Spring-Summer	Spring-Summer
Salix Willow	Spring-Summer	Summer	Spring-Summer[3]	Spring-Summer
Tamarix Tamarisk	Spring-Summer	Autumn	Spring-Summer	Spring[4]
Taxus Yew	Summer	Summer	Summer-Autumn	Spring[4]
Thuja Arborvitae	Spring & Autumn	Any time	Any time	Spring[4]
Tsuga Hemlock	Spring & Autumn	Any time	Any time	Spring-Summer[4]
Ulmus Elm	Spring-Summer	Spring-Summer	Spring-Summer[3]	Winter-Spring
Wisteria Wisteria	Summer-Winter[1]	Summer-Winter	Spring-Summer[3]	Spring
Zelkova Sawleaf zelkova	Spring-Summer	Spring-Summer	Any time	Winter-Spring

Key to Reference Numbers

[1] Pinch after flowers die, before new buds harden.
[2] Prune after flowering, before leaves appear.
[3] Bend after leaves are full size but while branches are still limber.
[4] Repot before new shoots appear.
[5] Repot just before flowering.
[6] Repot after flowering, before leaves open.

Care

Shelves and showcases

A bonsai becomes something to live with. Unlike a flower bed or border, it's permanent. With proper care it will in all likelihood outlive its owner.

As soon as you discover how very easy and enjoyable bonsai are, your collection will start to grow. What began as a tiny seedling in a miniature container will become a shelf of four or five junior-size trees. These in turn will develop into yet another shelf of larger and more handsome trees. As your interest and skill grow, so will your collection. You'll find that you are raising bonsai purely for the pleasure of handling a living plant form.

In your garden

If you have more than a couple of trees, you should set up a shelf or two for handling and for displaying specimens. Display shelves can be combined with a workbench or can be entirely separate.

All bonsai have the same basic requirements. They must have water, light, and good air circulation. They shouldn't be jammed so close that they deprive each other, yet they needn't be spread out so much that care becomes a chore.

Leave about a foot of space between the branches of specimens, certainly no less than 6 inches, depending on the size of the trees. Let them have some sun (morning is best), especially in the spring when new growth is sprouting. In full shade, the leaves of most plants will be pale and weak. Turn the containers every couple of weeks to let all sides of the foliage have the full benefit of watering, reflected light, and air currents. In containers that aren't turned, roots tend to grow to the side that isn't heated by the sun. The foliage, though, reaches toward the source of strongest light.

Trees that are kept too close to a wall often will develop withered branches in the back.

The simplest of shelves for holding or displaying bonsai can be made by setting a plank on two concrete blocks or some bricks.

In putting bonsai shelves against a light-colored outside wall away from trees, make sure they don't get too much sun. Between the sun's direct rays and those reflected from the wall, there can develop a great burning heat.

Slat benches and decks, either adjoining the house or in the garden, are good places for bonsai. They have something of an oriental look about them that is in harmony with the containers and the trees. Also, the space between the boards allows good air circulation between the pots and permits drainage without forming a lair for insects.

Larger bonsai are often too massive to keep on a shelf with other trees. The total weight may be too much for a single plank and can crack it and dump all the trees in a heap. If a shelf looks as if it's sagging in the middle, be sure to brace it. Remember that when plants have been freshly watered they are quite a bit heavier than when dry.

In your home

Bonsai are outdoor plants and should not be kept inside for more than a day or two. When they're in a house any longer, they suffer, most often from heat and the dryness of the air.

Bonsai enthusiasts have long been trying to develop successful indoor bonsai. Some have enjoyed great success; others have failed miserably. As yet, there's no tried-and-true method for bringing them inside, nor are there any tried-and-true plants that will absolutely not fail.

The thing to do is experiment. Many bonsai experts seem to have the most indoor success with tropicals and subtropicals such as camellia, gardenia, and heavenly bamboo. Other plants to try indoors are pyracantha, azalea, cotoneaster, ivy, hawthorn, myrtle, rosemary, Surinam cherry, Barbados cherry, and Singapore holly.

Whether you're trying for a full-time indoor bonsai or just bringing one in for temporary display, don't set a bonsai where it will receive direct sun, even through a window. Be certain it gets lots of light, though. Keep it away from hot-air ducts and radiators. Try opening a nearby window to provide fresh air circulation. Keep the room temperature below 70° and humidify the air, either with a standard humidifier or a pan of water standing nearby. Before bringing a bonsai indoors, water it and let it drain well for a couple of hours.

A *tokonoma*

In a traditional Japanese home — or a modern one that has even a little tradition carried into its design — there is an alcove known as a *tokonoma*. It is honored as the most important part of a home, for works of art are exhibited there.

The tokonoma is basically a platform raised a few inches above the regular floor level. A little larger than 3 by 6 feet, it's usually in a corner of the living room. Paintings, decorative scrolls, and calligraphy are hung against the wall at the back. On the platform are placed a flower arrangement, a piece of ceramic ware, a bronze incense burner, a bonsai, or some other very special object that has aesthetic value.

Locating such objects in an area such as this gives them special significance and draws attention to them. All of the above objects are not displayed together, since they would compete for attention, but certain of them are carefully chosen and arranged to complement one another or to emphasize one particular feature.

The same principle can be adapted to many areas in the home without the need for a tokonoma. For example, you can place a bonsai in front of a plain wall on a raised stand. On the wall, and a little to one side of the tree, you can hang a simple painting — one with colors that will not compete with any colors in the bonsai. Then you can add, on a lower stand, a fine piece of pottery. That's all — it's a simple grouping but one that is effective.

Stands and mats

Stands made especially for flower arrangements or bonsai display can be found in oriental stores. High tables are well suited for cascaded plants. The small, low, teak or rosewood tables with curved-under or stubby legs are good and can be found in stores that handle imported merchandise. A polished tree stump, with roots serving as legs and with a flat top, is expensive but handsome and carries through the natural appearance of the bonsai.

In general, the shape of the top of the stand or table should contrast with the shape of the container, and the height of the stand should harmonize with the height of the tree. Thus, a long, cascaded bonsai needs a high stand to allow full downward sweep of the foliage. A medium-high stand should be used for bonsai with straight, vertical trunks, and a broad, low stand is best for a grove of trees or a tree in the slanting style. Look at the photos of bonsai in this book for an idea of which stands go with which trees.

A mat or pad is usually placed between the container and the stand. It protects the surface of the stand and blends tree and container with the stand. Woven place mats in plain colors are used.

DISPLAY SHELVES for bonsai can be combined with a work center. Strong supports for shelves and some overhead protection are essential.

Display

Index

Boldface numbers refer to color photographs.

These national organizations will send you information about clubs in your area and about their own membership programs that include publications: American Bonsai Society, 228 Rosemont Ave., Erie, PA 16505; Bonsai Clubs International, 445 Blake St., Menlo Park, CA 94025.